The Creative Soul Within

REDISCOVER YOUR
IMAGINATION,
LET GO OF STRESS,
AND DEVELOP
THE CREATIVE GIFTS
GOD HAS GIVEN YOU

ZONDERVAN

The Creative Soul Within

© 2022 Zondervan

Requests for information should be addressed to:

Zondervan, 3900 Sparks Dr. SE, Grand Rapids, Michigan 49546

ISBN 978-0-310-46138-8 (audiobook)
ISBN 978-0-310-46137-1 (eBook)
ISBN 978-0-310-46135-7 (TP)

Art direction: Jennifer Showalter Greenwalt
Design: Kathy Mitchell, kathymitchelldesign.com
Photo credit: Susan Mohorn, stemandbranch.shop

Printed in India

22 23 24 25 26 REP 10 9 8 7 6 5 4 3 2 1

Contents

SECTION 2: God Made You to Connect

SECTION 3: God Made You for Joy

SECTION 4: God Made You for Growth

The truth is,
whether or
not you
feel creative,
you are.

Am I Creative?

In the midst of hectic day-to-day schedules, it's easy for our creative dreams and aspirations to fall by the wayside, or even become lost altogether. From managing calendars to fulfilling family, work, and household responsibilities—all of which are good and important—our creative spirits can sometimes fade into the background. Between all of this *doing*, there is still a part of us that longs to *make* something.

There is a unique creative instinct that still lives within each of us, and it's time to reawaken it.

The first step in reconnecting with that creativity is quieting the noise around us to allow ourselves time to be alone with our thoughts. So, what happens when we take the first big step of drowning out the sights and sounds of the day to focus on the creative task at hand and suddenly find ourselves... stuck?

Maybe this is where you are. You don't write stories. You don't make pottery. You don't draw or dance or design...

The truth is, regardless of whether you *feel* creative, you *are* creative. These are not empty words of encouragement. Rather, this is about who created you. You are the product of a wildly, unimaginably, profoundly creative God. You are His workmanship, Paul said in Ephesians 2:10: "For we are his workmanship, created in Christ Jesus for good works, which God prepared beforehand, that we should walk in them."

Another word for workmanship? *Masterpiece.* Imagine that. We are creations of a perfect God, and even with all our human flaws, we are made in His image. We are masterpieces made by a perfect Creator.

Michelangelo's *David* is known as the masterpiece of Renaissance sculpture. Some even call it the greatest sculpture the world has ever known. The piece, begun in 1501, wasn't completed until 1504. It is said that Michelangelo worked nonstop over the course of those three years to complete the impressive, seventeen-foot marble statue. But even one of the world's greatest artistic masterpieces is still only a replica of God's design.

We can only know true perfection in heaven, so anything we create here on earth is free from the pressure of being flawless. Thus, we can create in gratitude for the desires and abilities that God has given us. When the act of creating becomes an act of worship, there is no room left for worry.

> You are the product of a wildly, unimaginably, profoundly creative God.

> **That's what this journal is about. Remembering that we are creators.**

Also in Ephesians, Paul said we were chosen "in him before the foundation of the world" (1:4). If the world's greatest statue took less than four years to complete, and if God has been planning *your* design since *before* the world came to be, you must be impressive. Well-thought-out. In fact, Scripture says you are wonderfully and fearfully made (Psalm 139:14).

But does that make you creative?

Your Master Sculptor gave you much more than beauty and careful design. *He gave you life.* You are His masterpiece designed to move and breathe and think and, yes, create.

So, who cares if your sculpture doesn't look like a masterpiece? God gave you breath in your lungs, hands to hold tools, and a creative desire in your heart—these are gifts to be celebrated.

We create with God, the first and last and far-above-all-others Creative One. He is our Father; we inherited creativity from Him. We also create with each other. All of us masterpieces walking around on this earth—we work together. We support each other.

That's what this journal is about. Remembering that we are creators. Expressing gratitude for our creative gifts. Connecting with God, and each other, as we awaken the creative soul within.

X   THE CREATIVE SOUL WITHIN

God Made You to Make

On the creative process, on God's creative process, on finding your way into creating.

Take a Chance and Begin

In the beginning, God created the heavens and the earth. The earth was without form and void, and darkness was over the face of the deep.

GENESIS 1:1–2

Isn't there something special about the beginning of things? A new birth. A new job. A new home. The beginning is full of hope and excitement, full of wonder for what is to come. The thing is, you don't know the ending. Not really. You can guess that you'll stay in your home for the next fifteen years, but who knows? It's often this unknowing that keeps us from getting started.

God *knew* where His world would end up–in imperfection and sin, in darkness and despair. Still, He picked the creation day and began.

Buy the seeds.
Write the page.
Take the class.
Cut the fabric.

You don't know where your creative endeavors will end. That's the best part! The thrill of starting something new, the anticipation of where the project will lead, the discovery of self along the way. The creative process is just that: a process. It's not just about the outcome. It's about the

journey, which invites us to learn about ourselves, others, and God with every step. If your feelings are walking the line between intimidation and excitement, that's okay, because this allows you to be vulnerable with God and embrace the openness that comes with taking a leap, even if you don't know where you're going to land.

And remember, you are not on this path alone. You may not know where this endeavor will end, but you do know who's on your side—not only the Master Creator but the people in your life who love and support you as well. So even if the project goes a little haywire somewhere in the middle, if the garden doesn't take off, or if the book takes a few more years than you expected, you won't face these hardships by yourself.

So why not take a chance and begin?

Buy the seeds. Write the page. Take the class. Cut the fabric. Whatever's on your heart, take your first steps toward achieving it today. The beginning is beautiful; don't hesitate to embrace it—the joy, the excitement, the wonder. Breathe in those feelings deeply; savor the joie de vivre of finally saying yes and taking a chance on something new.

REFLECT

Today's activity is all about you. Other prompts will ask you to try something new or something outside your wheelhouse, but this one is about embracing the thing you've had on your heart for a while now . . . the creative work you've put off for a better time.

Guess what? Your time is today.

In the space below, make a list of your first steps toward achieving your creative goal. This doesn't have to be exhaustive, but it should be specific. What do you need to buy? What time do you need to set aside? How much? Who can help you? When will you talk to them?

Make your list and get started.

_____

_____

_____

_____

_____

_____

_____

_____

_____

_____

_____

_____

_____

_____

_____

Step Back and Celebrate

God saw that it was good.

GENESIS 1:12

During those first days when God created the world, He made a point to stop several times throughout the process and admire what He had just done. Scripture records seven instances when God stepped back from the creative process to see that His work was "good."

How often do you celebrate what you've done? When you finish a project at work, do you have a party? Do you at least pat yourself on the back? And no, this isn't figurative. You should literally, joyfully, and in real time celebrate your achievements.

Celebrate the fact that you did something good.

This is part of the creative process, as taught to us by our creative Father. Do a thing. Stop. Notice it. Celebrate.

Yet too often, the cycle looks more like this: Do a thing. Do another thing. Repeat . . . to the point of utter exhaustion.

No wonder we're missing joy. But what if we changed our pattern and broke the cycle? What if every time we accomplished something—at home, at work, at church—we took a little break to celebrate before jumping to the next activity? To see that it is *good*?

You can celebrate simple tasks: *I finished reading a book. Let me celebrate with a favorite coffee!* The more effort you put in, be sure to stop and celebrate *big*. As your effort increases, allow the celebration to follow suit.

EMBRACE

Plan a celebration party—yes, a full-fledged p-a-r-t-y!—for a milestone you were proud to hit over this past year. It doesn't matter how long ago it was. Did you finish a degree? Did you head up a project at work? Did you finish a painting? Did you follow through with your commitment to walk every day for a month? Whatever it was, plan a party that says, "Hey, I did good!"

SUPPLIES:

- *Invitations (optional)*
- *Cake (your choice!)*
- *Paper plates*
- *Banner or bouquet*
- *Napkins*

If you prefer, you can keep things simple and just enjoy a slice of cake after dinner with your family. After all, the people around your table probably had a lot to do with why you finished in the first place. The main thing is to call your work *good*—because God is working in you, and what you do together is worth celebrating.

Say It Out Loud

For he spoke, and it came to be; he
commanded, and it stood firm.
PSALM 33:9

When God created the world, He spoke
it into existence. Pretty incredible, right?
Also, pretty hard to relate to.

Is there anything in life that allows us
to just say the words and it is so? "We
will have chicken tortellini for dinner" . . .
and it comes to be. Now that would be
incredible.

While we don't have God's power to
speak things into being, we do have the gift of prayer. Here's what Jesus
said: "Ask, and it will be given to you; seek, and you will find; knock,
and it will be opened to you" (Matthew 7:7). God spoke the world into
existence, and just like our Creator, we can speak life into our dreams–by
offering them to God.

Does this mean we can ask God to make us phenomenal painters,
songwriters, bakers, or builders overnight? Absolutely not. Rather, bringing our creative dreams to God in the act of humble prayer is to ask Him

When we are brave enough to speak our dreams out loud and vulnerable enough to allow God to guide them, we open ourselves up to a journey far more beautiful than we could have fathomed all on our own.

to guide the journey. When we share the desires of our hearts with God through prayer, we are exercising vulnerability and being open to what our God who sees, knows, and loves us will do with our dreams. The more we practice sharing our dreams with God–and asking for His intercession in them–the more we will be able to see His loving presence along the journey as we aspire to fulfill our creative endeavors.

I want to speak a new language.

I want to coach a team.

I want to lead a Bible study.

Most important: *God, how can these desires of my heart be used to honor You?*

Whatever dream you have floating about your heart, whatever creative endeavor you haven't yet seen come true, speak it out loud today in prayer. Then keep going: speak it out loud again. To a friend. To your spouse. To a colleague. To your boss. The bolder and more persistent you are, the more you will find the support and resources you need to see

your dream come true. When we are brave enough to speak our dreams aloud and vulnerable enough to allow God to guide them, we open ourselves up to a journey far more beautiful than we could have fathomed all on our own.

INSPIRE

Before you can say it out loud, you have to define what your dream is. Maybe you have several. In the space provided draw a dream web. This can look however you want. One suggestion is to draw small clouds with your dreams written inside each. Or you might draw one big cloud with your dreams written inside and the words "ask," "seek," and "knock" written all around the edges.

Once you're done, choose at least one dream to pray about with persistence over the next seven days. Then choose one person you will share your dream with. *Say the words out loud.*

Work with Your Hands

But now, O LORD, you are our Father; we are the clay, and you are our potter; we are all the work of your hand.

ISAIAH 64:8

Sometimes God spoke things into existence; sometimes He worked with His hands.

We can understand why, right? There are some activities where you just have to get your hands dirty. You have to get involved. You want to be as close to the creation of the object as possible, not missing a moment of its making.

What did God work on this closely? You.

"We are all the work of [His] hand" (Isaiah 64:8).

Another scripture says, "For you formed my inward parts; you knitted me together in my mother's womb" (Psalm 139:13).

Handmade gifts are always special, but what's doubly special about a handmade *knitted* gift is that you know the maker's hands touched every single weave. Their fingers were part of every loop, every pull around, every stitch.

God's hands were this involved in making you. It's amazing to consider.

While you were inside the protective womb, God was busy stitching you together, weaving in and out, pulling above and around, carefully choosing your colors and texture and design. No doubt smiling and calling you good while His work came together—slowly, one stitch at a time.

The next time you use your hands to create, imagine God's hands working quietly and carefully on you. Realize what a beautiful gift you are to this world. The work of Master hands.

CREATE

Do you knit? If you don't, you're likely to know a friend who does. Your task this week is to contact that friend, have a fun conversation about how you want to try something new, and ask for help on a small project: knitting a washcloth!

If you find that your friends are just as inexperienced as you are when it comes to knitting, there are tons of accessible instructional videos to be found online for you to learn the new task together.

This is one of the simplest projects to start with when it comes to knitting (or crochet). You'll need help casting on, but once you're set, it's a simple, repetitive (and somewhat healing) motion. You'll catch on, and once you're done, every time you use it, you'll have a tangible reminder of how closely involved God was in making you.

SUPPLIES:

- *Yarn (pick colors that make you smile!)*
- *Knitting needles (can be borrowed)*
- *Coffee/dessert (for you and your friend)*

Right outside of our
front doors we can
find a tapestry created
to sustain life itself.

Share What You Make

The LORD . . . who formed the earth . . . did not
create it empty, he formed it to be inhabited!

ISAIAH 45:18

While most works of art appeal to one or two senses at a time—the colors of a painting that excite the eyes, the melodic notes of a symphony that wash over the eardrums—God has given us a great creation that ignites all of our human senses at once. Right outside of our front doors we can find a tapestry created to sustain life itself.

When He breathed life into Adam and Eve, "God blessed them. And God said to them, 'Be fruitful and multiply and fill the earth and subdue it'" (Genesis 1:28). He invited them to share in His creation of the very source of physical life—planet Earth—offering them His beautiful plant life for sustenance and entrusting His animals to their dominion. God wanted the earth—the world *He* made—to be inhabited, cared for, and enjoyed.

In order to benefit from the earth, we must also tend to and care for it. Just as we're called to be good stewards of God's beautiful earthly creation, we are also invited to delight in the bounties of this earth with gratitude—and in community.

What better way to honor the great gift God shared with us than to

celebrate it over a meal with others? Whether it's a casual picnic beneath a sunset in a park, or a delectable meal enjoyed over candlelight, we are invited to delight in the gifts of God's earthly bounty by sharing meals with loved ones and strangers alike.

CONNECT

Nothing makes people feel more wanted or welcome than an open door. This week, be intentional about opening your door to someone who might need it. Look for someone sitting alone on the pew, or eating lunch every day by himself, or walking alone in your neighborhood.

Invite them into your home. Maybe even invite a few additional friends to make it a proper dinner party. Prepare a special meal—something out of the ordinary and, perhaps, artistic. Curate a playlist for background music. Create pretty place cards. Allow your guests to sit at your table and share what you made. You might even pull out that pretty crystal you inherited from Aunt Mabel. Remember, your home is a gift to be inhabited—and shared!

Light Up the Day

"You are the light of the world. A city set on a hill cannot be hidden."

MATTHEW 5:14

Have you ever noticed how artwork on display in a museum or gallery seems to sparkle with life in a way that reproduced images of those same pieces never could? Almost as if the colors dance on the canvas in a choreography of vibrancy and vitality. While great works of art are preserved through careful maintenance, the lighting is what allows our eyes to appreciate the fullness of their beauty. Gallerists consult with lighting experts and pay for special bulbs, lenses, and filters, which are placed strategically throughout their spaces, so the pieces can be seen in the best light, literally.

The lighting helps you distinguish nuances of color you can't see as easily, or at all. It controls glare and brings out the subtleties of the stroke work; according to the experts, the lighting is what brings the work to life. It's what allows us to see the true and total beauty of the artist's creation.

Jesus called His people "the light of the world" (Matthew 5:14). In a way, it's like we're those special bulbs, and God has strategically placed

us in a position of prominence "on a hill."

Today, think of yourself as that light (because you are!). You were designed to draw out the best in others, to highlight their beauty, to show off their full potential.

Living this out is simple: notice the best in others and call attention to it. "You have the kindest personality. Did you know that?" "You work so hard every day, and we appreciate you." "I just love your smile." The little things you notice might just make for the brightest moments of someone else's day.

Think of someone at your work, in your home, or at your church who might need a little pick-me-up. How can you brighten his or her day?

One idea is to turn their name into an acrostic poem. First, spell their name below, writing each letter on its own line. Then, using each letter once, write something positive about that person. What do they do well? What are their best qualities? What do they contribute to your life? You can try rhyming the lines, but you don't have to.

Once you're done, copy your acrostic onto a card and mail it to that person. What better way to light up their day?

_____

_____

_____

_____

_____

_____

_____

_____

You were designed to
draw out the best in
others, to highlight their
beauty, to show off
their full potential.

Find Your Team

The LORD possessed me at the beginning of his
work, the first of his acts of old.

PROVERBS 8:22

When we think of the creative greats—
Edison, Disney, Shakespeare, van
Gogh—we don't remember, or even
know, the names of the people behind
these geniuses. The ones who likely
supported and inspired them to keep
creating, keep going, no matter what.

Where can you find the names of an
artist's team today? Read the acknowl-
edgments that accompany their work.
You'll find editors and friends, family members and fans. You'll read the
names of dozens, sometimes hundreds, of people who assisted the artist, in one way or another, to finish their work.

In assembling your dream team, what better example is there than
Jesus Himself? While He could have sought out religious, political,

> In assembling your dream team, who better to look toward as an example of the discernment exercised when doing so than Jesus Himself?

or social figures with substantial clout to legitimize His teachings, He instead trusted in God's vision and sought out those with unique spiritual gifts. The meek and the troubled, the sinners and the scorned. Those who were inspired to support His mission and also stood to benefit from it. Those who, in the act of feeding others, could be fed themselves.

If even Jesus had a team in place to support and work with Him in bringing the good news to the world, who are we to think we could ever accomplish our creative endeavors alone? Who are the people in your life with unique spiritual gifts that you might call upon to strengthen your creative endeavors? How might you give to them in return?

EMBRACE

Do you know your team? Perhaps you need to be more intentional about seeking members to join it: people who can pray for you, check up on you, read your work while it's in progress, lift you up when you're ready to quit.

Today, start building your team by making a web of Post-it Notes. Write the different roles you think you'll need to accomplish your work: prayer warrior, previewer, idea bouncer, etc. Then write the names of friends who could fill these roles. Post the notes on your mirror, and pray for the roles you still need filled. Write names down as you figure them out. You're on your way to finding your team!

Go one step further by examining your gifts as a team member. What supporting role do you play in the creative endeavors that your loved ones take on? Just as you ask your friends to pour into you, be ready to pour into them in return.

SUPPLIES:
- Post-it Notes

Give Something New a Try

He has filled them with skill to do every sort of work . . . by any sort of workman or skilled designer.

EXODUS 35:35

When it came time to build the tabernacle–God's home among His people, the Israelites–He could have spoken the holy tent into existence, just as He did at creation. He could have whispered the words "Let there be . . . ," and there it would have been.

Instead, He enlisted the efforts of people.

Not only that, but He gifted people with the abilities He wanted them to use: "He has filled them with skill to do every sort of work done by an engraver or by a designer or by an embroiderer . . . or by a weaver" (Exodus 35:35). Whatever needed to be done, God gave them the ability to see it through.

There is comfort in pursuing endeavors that we feel equipped to handle, so our abilities often influence the opportunities we seek out. But what if we allowed a need–whether it's a need we observe in our community or within our own hearts–to reveal abilities we didn't even know we had? What if we signed up, in faith, to try the work before we knew we could actually do it?

> **What if we signed up, in faith, to try the work before we knew we could actually do it?**

Sure, there will be lots of unknowns, but here's what you can count on: if God wants you to do something, He can and will give you what you need to see the job through. There may be bumps along the way and the outcome may not look the way you'd envisioned—it might even look like a failure to worldly eyes—but if you approach it with a humble heart that trusts the Lord, the *work* will be *good*. Remember, it's about the journey, not the outcome.

Sign up. Show up. Give it a try. You never know what abilities are living within until you give them a chance to shine.

CREATE

Discovering new abilities is exciting. It brings freshness to our days, shaking us out of our routine. And it invites us to recycle the knowledge and abilities we've gained through other experiences, applying them to something new.

This week's craft mimics that process. You're taking old paper–paper grocery sacks work perfectly here–and turning it into something useful: a recycled paper basket! More detailed instructions can be found online, but here are the basics: (1) cut paper strips of the same length and width, (2) weave the first strip, (3) weave the base, (4) fold to create the bottom, and (5) continue to weave over and under, using a clothespin to secure the weave as you work. When the basket is the size you want, simply use glue to secure the top!

SUPPLIES:

- *Recycled paper*
- *Clothespin*
- *Scissors*
- *Craft glue*

It's Okay to Start Again

So the Lord said, "I will blot out man
whom I have created."

GENESIS 6:7

Acts 3:19–20 says, "Repent therefore, and turn back, that your sins may be blotted out, that times of refreshing may come from the presence of the Lord." In confessing our sins with a conciliatory heart, we are given the gift of a pure one. After the dark night, the day is made new.

Just as our imperfect human nature ensures that we'll need a reset from time to time, your creative endeavors may need a fresh start too. It's not that you haven't tried. It's not that you haven't put in your best effort. But sometimes the obstacles are meant to serve as signs: you should turn here, make a change . . . instead of barreling down the same road and perhaps forcing something that isn't working.

> Just as our imperfect human nature ensures that we'll need a reset from time to time, your creative endeavors may need a fresh start too.

The definition of insanity—you know it? Doing the same thing over and over, expecting different results.

The precursor to burnout? Insanity.

If this is where you are today—stuck in the middle of something that feels like a dead end—prayerfully consider whether it's time for a change. Maybe it's your job. Maybe it's the side gig you can't quite get to take off.

Vincent van Gogh came to this same crossroad. He tried selling art. He tried teaching school. He even tried preaching. Then, one day, he picked up a canvas and painted as he stood by the sea. He tried something new. This means pivoting, taking a chance, turning your back on something old.

Who knows? This new road might be the one God was leading you toward all along.

IMAGINE

Have any experience working with pottery? Or maybe you've seen someone else work at the wheel? If so, you know the potter can lump up the ball of clay and begin again at any point when he or she realizes the project isn't going as planned.

This week, your task is to find a friend—or take your child!—and book an afternoon at a pottery studio. Some studios only allow you to paint, so search for one in your area that also allows you to sculpt the clay.

As you create (and, perhaps, re-create) together, realize that even if you have to start over, nothing is wasted—not time, not materials. They're just applied to something new!

What's Broken Can Be Restored

"Thus says the Lord GOD . . . I will cause the cities to be inhabited, and the waste places shall be rebuilt."

EZEKIEL 36:33

Sometimes you will need to completely pivot. Start over. Take a new road. Other times, you simply need to pick up the broken pieces in front of you and rebuild.

God modeled this for us when He promised to rebuild the cities of His people. Despite His people careening into sin again, He didn't start over with another flood and only save those who were worthy of favor in His eyes. Instead, God took what remained and restored it–from something wasteful and broken into something beautiful and functional once more.

> The Repairer.
> The Restorer.
> This is who
> God is for us,
> His people.

Thus, He was called "the repairer of the breach, the restorer of streets to dwell in" (Isaiah 58:12). The Repairer. The Restorer. This is who God is for us, His people. And with His help, this is who we can be for the people and projects of our day too.

Is there a relationship you've given up on?

Maybe it's time to repair the breach that caused you to drift apart. Is there a project you've stopped investing in? Perhaps it's time to restore the pieces that have been left lying around.

Before you quit something altogether, seek God's guidance: Is this something that can be restored?

EXPLORE

In Japan there is an art form known as *kintsugi*. Translated as "golden joinery," kintsugi is the act of putting broken pieces of pottery back together with an adhesive and gold. The idea behind it is embracing–even highlighting–imperfections, ultimately changing our perception: what's broken becomes beautiful.

This week, try "the art of repair" for yourself. Visit your nearest thrift store and find a ceramic piece that draws your eye. When you get home, place your ceramic piece in a paper bag before (carefully) breaking it. (You want large enough pieces that you can glue them back together.) Then begin the process of restoration, turning your broken pieces into something beautiful!

SUPPLIES:
- *Kintsugi glue (adhesive mixed with golden powder)*
- *Ceramic pot, cup, etc.*
- *Paintbrush*

Seek the Vision

Then Jesus laid his hands on his eyes again; and he opened his eyes, his sight was restored, and he saw everything clearly.

MARK 8:25

We have talked about taking a chance and getting started. About believing in your dreams. About forming a team to help you achieve them. About pivoting or repairing the broken pieces as you encounter obstacles along the way.

But we've made the assumption that you know what you want to do.

Maybe you do, and that's a gift to be thankful for. But what if you don't?

In Mark 8, a blind man was brought to Jesus. Jesus took him outside of the village and began the process of restoring his sight. First, He spit on the blind man's eyes and laid hands on him. The man could see but not well. Then Jesus laid His hands on the man again, and this time the man "saw everything clearly" (vv. 22–25).

This miracle was physical, but often the problem of lacking vision isn't. Sometimes we can see very clearly what's right in front of us, but we fail to see what we were made to do, what our gifts are, and how we should use our talents to act on our dreams.

Just as the blind man sought healing from Jesus, anyone lacking vision—of any kind—can do the same. Read the story again: this healing is even for those who have a general idea but can only see the fuzzy details. The dream isn't yet clear. Seek Jesus and ask for His miraculous touch to enhance your vision.

REFLECT

To heal the blind man in Mark 8, Jesus spit on his eyes before laying hands on him. In another passage, Jesus healed a man's eyes by spitting on the ground and making mud (John 9:6).

The path to vision, to cleansing, to healing isn't always what we think. Take, for instance, the path to refining our skin. It's not just clean water and soap that you need; it's mud! This week, mix up your own mud mask and apply it to your face and neck for ten minutes before rinsing. While letting the ingredients do their work, think about Jesus cleansing and renewing you in ways you may never understand.

SUPPLIES:

- *1 teaspoon clay mask powder*
- *1 teaspoon warm water (add more if needed)*
- *1 drop of essential oil (your choice)*
- *Optional exfoliant: sea salt or sugar*

Sometimes we can see very clearly what's right in front of us, but we fail to see what we were made to do.

Not When, but Now

Behold, I am the servant of the Lord; let it be to me according to your word.

LUKE 1:38

I'll make that when I have more time. I should've tried that when I could have learned more easily. We have all kinds of excuses for why we won't do, try, make, go, visit, write, draw, create.

Most of those excuses involve the word "when." The best time to approach this venture is either in the future or sometime in the past. In both cases the dream is discarded because the mindset we hold is *when* instead of *now.* A yes is not a true yes if it is conditional.

When Mary was approached by the Holy Spirit to be the mother of Jesus, it would have made sense for her to have sought a better time: *Can't we do this when I'm married? That way I am spared the humiliation of a pre-wedding pregnancy, forfeiting my reputation and relationships with nearly everyone I love.*

Instead, Mary asked one question: "How will this be, since I am a virgin?" And once she heard the plan, she obliged and said, "Let it be to me according to your word" (Luke 1:34, 38). Mary's *yes*, also known as Mary's *fiat*, which in Latin means "let it be done," was not conditional. She received God's blessing without hesitation or concern for circumstance.

Whatever God's plan is for you, when He reveals it, caution yourself against asking too many questions, lest fear talk you out of trying. You might ask *how*, but even if it requires great risk, if this is God's dream for you, He will be with you.

So, what is your *fiat*? To what great adventure are you being called? The time to say yes is now.

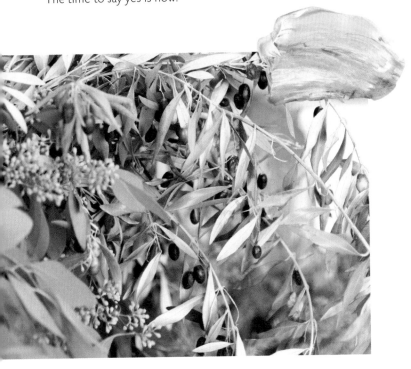

PLAN

Creative ventures often take time to develop, but be patient as God guides you along. Small investments each day–this is how we achieve our dreams!

In the space below, draw a weekly calendar. This can be simple: seven boxes with the day of the week at the top. Below each day, sketch ideas of what you can do to make small investments toward your dream. Aim for fifteen to thirty minutes about five days per week. Spend this time cooking, writing, drawing, reading, painting, exploring, sketching, gardening, learning . . . whatever God puts on your heart.

A yes is not a true yes if it is conditional.

Walk on Water

Jesus looked at them and said, "With man this is impossible, but with God all things are possible."

MATTHEW 19:26

Mary's only question, after being told she would carry the Son of God, was reasonable: How? It didn't make sense. It had never been done before. It seemed impossible.

Read through the Bible, and you'll find that God's dreams often are impossible.

> David defeated Goliath.
> Esther, a Jewish orphan, became a Persian queen.
> Gideon's three hundred men defeated an army of thousands.
> Peter walked on water.

Each of these individuals began by saying yes to God, and then they took that very first step. Following their examples, we, too, can find courage to do the impossible when we humble ourselves to God's will and entrust ourselves to His provision.

Imagine what it must have felt like for Peter as Jesus called to him

from a great distance, the wild storm swirling around them. Had Peter focused on the far-off horizon, the task of walking on water might have felt insurmountable. But, in fixing his eyes on Jesus, he was able to take that very first step, and each step thereafter. It was only when Peter's fear began to take control that he started to sink—and Jesus saved him from drowning.

The art of walking on water is not about racing toward the horizon. It's about taking one step, followed by another, along a journey mapped by God's grace.

With this in mind, how are you going to start your project? This is a reasonable question to work out with God through prayer. What are your first steps going to be? As He provides clarity, tweak your schedule. Make the phone calls. Buy the supplies. The key is to take it one day, one step, one act of obedience at a time.

Eventually, you'll get there—standing smack in the middle of the dream, looking around in wonder and with gratitude. Like Peter, you may just find yourself doing the impossible.

GROW

Growing a plant from seed requires trust in the process. You can't see what's happening beneath the surface, and it seems impossible: Can something so tiny produce flowers, vegetables, even trees? If you're faithful to do your part, God will give the growth (1 Corinthians 3:6).

This week, try starting a plant from seed. If it's cold outside, select an easy indoor plant (see the list below); if it's warm and sunny, then choose a plant of your choice. As you witness your seeds' first sprouts and, later, first blooms, thank God for the growth.

The art of walking on water is . . . about taking one step, followed by another, along a journey mapped by God's grace.

SUPPLIES:

- *Container (any kind, but with drainage holes)*
- *Potting soil*
- *Seeds (peace lilies, lavender, herbs)*

God Made You to Connect

On connecting with others, on relationships, on being intentional and creative in the ways we build them.

Love Is a Treasure

"It is not good that the man should be alone; I will make him a helper fit for him."

GENESIS 2:18

God didn't intend for His created people to be alone. This doesn't mean every person God made should be married—some people are called to singleness and live full and beautiful lives in community—but this is His design for many. And it was the first relationship God established after He finished creating the world.

"The LORD God caused a deep sleep to fall upon the man, and while he slept took one of his ribs and closed up its place with flesh. And the rib that the LORD God had taken from the man he made into a woman and brought her to the man" (Genesis 2:21–22). God carefully, meticulously—with the precision of a surgeon—created the woman whom Adam was to spend his life with. This woman far surpassed anything in creation

Adam had seen before: "This at last is bone of my bones and flesh of my flesh" (v. 23).

At last.

Love between husband and wife is a treasure. It's worth *far* more than the cost of her diamond engagement ring, the value of any home they might purchase, or the money they will earn throughout their lifetime. As Song of Solomon says, "If a man offered for love all the wealth of his house, he would be utterly despised" (8:7).

Yet isn't marriage one of the easiest relationships to take for granted?

God didn't intend for us to be alone, nor did He intend for us to forget: the one we love was carefully, meticulously, mercifully brought into our lives by our Creator.

> God didn't intend for His created people to be alone.

IMAGINE

Song of Solomon contains an oft quoted verse about love: "Set me as a seal upon your heart, as a seal upon your arm, for love is strong as death" (8:6). This seal, often worn as a ring, was used to show ownership. The wearer would press his seal into the object he wished to display as his own.

If you're married, or if you and your significant other are preparing for marriage, use the space provided to design a seal that represents you and your spouse. You can include anything: your initials, your wedding date, a favorite vacation spot. Think about what connects you and makes you unique as a couple.

If you're single, design a seal that represents what you hope to offer the world as a future married person or as a person who is called to singleness. How will you honor God in this role? What unique gifts will you have to offer, and how would you like God to prepare you for this future?

Imagine this seal pressed into the fabric of the life you're building—either as a person living in virtuous singleness for the Lord, or as a husband or wife within a marriage that honors God.

New Life Is a Miracle

Listen to your father who gave you life. Let her who bore you rejoice.

PROVERBS 23:22, 25

Creation of life didn't end with Eve in Genesis 2. God, in His infinite and inexplicable grace, allowed His creatures to then join in the life-making process. Adam and Eve, by their union, created a son.

This pattern of coming together in love and producing new life is the stuff of miracles. It is God-designed and therefore divine.

Yet, our modern world often views the miracle of life as commonplace, ordinary, and in some cases a burden. Have we forgotten what an extraordinary gift this new-life-making ability really is?

One man, one woman: the two together become one *more*.

Now, men and women celebrate a father-and-mother relationship and together with their children model the holy family of Jesus, Mary, and Joseph. Parents learn together how to raise children who walk in the ways of the One who created them all: "These words that I command you today shall be on your heart. You shall teach them diligently to your children, and shall talk of them when you sit in your house, and when you walk by the way, and when you lie down, and when you rise"

(Deuteronomy 6:6–7).

Parents aren't perfect like our heavenly Father, but they are meant to be respected. And when they're committed to following Him—the One who created us all—they should be valued, listened to, and doubly revered.

REFLECT

Do you know how your parents met? If your parents are still with you, spend time this week reconnecting and give them the chance to relive the details. Ask them what it felt like to fall in love all those years ago. If they've already gone home to heaven, call to mind what you remember about their relationship. How did you observe the love shared between them?

There's a possibility that this exercise might touch some wounds, but remember, Jesus touched wounds in order to heal them. Even in suffering there is beauty to be found. The relationship between a mother and a father greatly influences the lives of their children. How do you see God's hand in your parents' story? How, in turn, do

This pattern of coming together in love and producing new life is the stuff of miracles.

you see God's hand in yours?

If you have children, do your kids know how their parents met? In the space below write it down for them. Tell the story of God's hand in both of your lives and all He did to bring you together. If you need more space, find paper or open a new document and keep writing. When it's time, share your story with the new life He gave you the ability to create.

_____

_____

_____

_____

_____

_____

_____

_____

_____

_____

_____

Siblings Really Are a Gift

A friend loves at all times, and a brother is born for adversity.

PROVERBS 17:17

It's strange, or maybe it's not: when you look for good examples of sibling relationships in the Bible, they're hard to find.

Cain and Abel—not a good place to start. Then there's Jacob, who lied and stole from his brother, Esau. Jacob's sons dumped their brother Joseph in a well before selling him to foreign traders.

One of the only good Old Testament stories we find about brothers isn't about biological brothers at all. David and Jonathan were friends who became like brothers—closer even. The Bible describes their relationship this way: "Jonathan became one in spirit with David, and he loved him as himself" (1 Samuel 18:1 sc).

Siblings—the ones with whom we live and share DNA, the ones we should love the most—might also be the ones who drive us the craziest. They may also be the ones who know us the best because we allow them to see us at our worst.

We choose our friends, but our siblings are given to us by God.

To grow up under the same roof with siblings–to know one another as we change and mature over the years–is an incredible gift. We choose our friends, but our siblings are given to us by God. We may not appreciate this gift in our younger years, but as we grow older, we begin to recognize the special bond between brothers and sisters. After all, you're the only people in the whole world who share the unique memories–good, bad, or bittersweet–of what it was like to grow up with your family.

PLAY

David and Jonathan had a special relationship. With as many songs as David wrote (see the book of Psalms), surely some of them looked back fondly on the brother-like bond they shared.

Let the childhood you shared with your siblings run through your head like an old home movie. Watch the grainy images of days gone by. What sibling memories are you thankful for? Sure, you might have to sift through some not-so-great memories, but hindsight might reveal some of the difficult times to be the ones

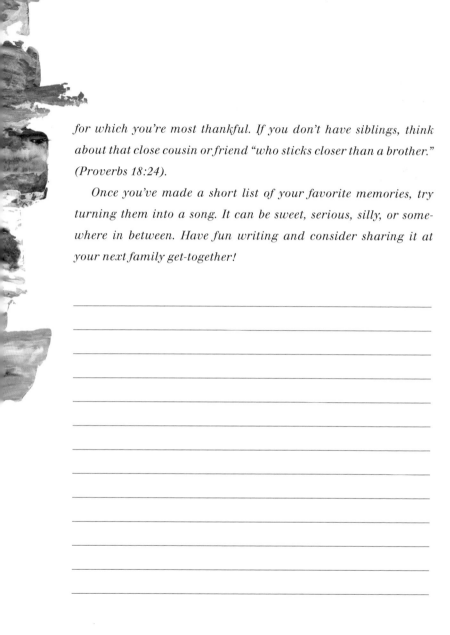

for which you're most thankful. If you don't have siblings, think about that close cousin or friend "who sticks closer than a brother." (Proverbs 18:24).

Once you've made a short list of your favorite memories, try turning them into a song. It can be sweet, serious, silly, or somewhere in between. Have fun writing and consider sharing it at your next family get-together!

_____

_____

_____

_____

_____

_____

_____

_____

_____

_____

_____

_____

_____

Grandparents Can Be a Crown

Grandchildren are the crown of the aged.

PROVERBS 17:6

A special bond exists between grandparents and grandchildren. Proverbs alludes to this with the reminder that "grandchildren are the crown of the aged" (17:6). They make the grandparents proud, they make them hold their heads a little higher and show off with a broad smile on their faces.

What about grandchildren? Are they just as excited to talk about their grandparents? Do they show off pictures and tell stories of their grandparents' courage or accomplishments? Just as our fallen world often devalues the biblical strengths of humility and generosity, it also tends to discard the elder generations who are deserving of the most honor. We get caught up in the newest notions, failing to seek the wisdom that only age and experience can offer.

In most cases the relationship between grandparents and grandchildren isn't exactly reciprocal. The Bible doesn't say "grandparents are the crown of the young." It does, however, talk about knowing and attending to your grandparents' needs (1 Timothy 5:4).

Instead of just caring *for* our elder generations, what if we cared *about* them a little more? What if we listened to their stories with as much energy and excitement as they give to ours? Maybe we could learn from their mistakes. Maybe we'd realize how cool they are. Maybe we'd step outside of ourselves and come to humbly and gratefully appreciate the sacrifices their generation made in order to pave a path for ours. Maybe we'd see that grandparents can and should be a crown.

INSPIRE

If you are so blessed to have the elder generations of your family still with you, call a grandparent this week and ask about their

life. What are they proud of? What funny stories can they share? What did they learn the hard way? What life advice do they have for you?

If you don't have grandparents around, contact a local nursing home or eldercare facility and ask if you can spend some time with someone who doesn't receive regular visits from loved ones. The elderly are often forgotten in our society, and old age can be incredibly lonely. Perhaps you can be an adoptive grandchild to someone who has boundless wisdom to share.

Before you end the conversation, ask for their favorite Bible verse. Write it below or mock up a simple postcard design around it. Once you have an idea in mind, cut a postcard-sized rectangle from cardstock and create your designed Bible verse. Mail it to your grandparent when you finish!

SUPPLIES:

- Cardstock
- Envelope
- Stamp
- Colored pencils or markers (optional)
- Scissors

Instead of just caring *for* our elder generations, what if we cared *about* them a little more?

The Family You Choose

A man of many companions may come to ruin, but there is a friend who sticks closer than a brother.

PROVERBS 18:24

In many ways, friends become our chosen family.

Philia is the Greek word for close friendship, or brotherly love, and the Bible places enormous importance on this kind of love. As we're assured in John 15:13, "Greater love has no one than this: to lay down one's life for one's friends" (NIV).

Best friends are truly one of God's greatest gifts. Like all of God's blessings, they are freely given but require that we tend to and care for them lest we squander the riches that have been bestowed upon us. In order to *have* a good friend, we must *be* a good friend.

Good friends don't just support us in times of need and laugh with us in times of joy. They also challenge us to be the people that God calls us to be; they help us become the best versions of ourselves. A good best friend will tell you the truth even when you don't want to hear it. They will help you see when you are off track—or when you are right on track but are scared and considering giving up. They will hold you accountable, but they will not leave you to clean up your messes on your own.

You need this kind of support if you're going to be any kind of creative.

It's also important to be aware of the fact that we become like the people with whom we surround ourselves. For better or worse, we are influenced by those around us, so it's vital to invest in friendships that are edifying and honor the Lord.

If you have found this friend—maybe even in a family member—be grateful. Let them know you appreciate them and understand their value. Most of all, be the kind of friend they need in return.

CONNECT

Write the name of your best friend: _____ .

In what way has he or she supported you over the last year, whether in your job, with your family, in your creative endeavors, or in general? Write your response below; be as specific as possible.

Write a thank-you letter to this friend, mentioning some of the specific reasons you're grateful for him or her. You can mail the letter or read it to your friend.

SUPPLIES:

- *Paper*
- *Envelope (optional)*
- *Stamp (optional)*

How Caring for Animals Can Help Us Grow

God blessed them and said to them, "Be fruitful and increase in number; fill the earth and subdue it. Rule over the fish in the sea and the birds in the sky and over every living creature that moves on the ground."

GENESIS 1:28 NIV

While God decreed that humankind would rule over the plants and animals, we are called to care for all living things with the dignity and respect with which God cares for us.

Owning a pet can be a great way to practice the essential art of taking care of dependent living things. When we invite pets into our home, we don't only invite their cuddles and companionship, we also invite the responsibility of caring for them. They force us to take a break and step outside for periods of time to be in tune to their needs. In turn, they help us laugh; they help us play. For just a few moments a day, when we delay our own needs to take care of theirs, they can boost our mood and give us the energy we need to keep going.

In addition to the immediate benefits of companionship and the practical development of responsibility, animals can also foster creativity.

Pets have served as inspiration for stories for as long as Old Testament books have been around. In the New Testament, Jesus told many stories about animals—sheep, sparrows, doves, dogs, snakes. We learn from animals. They help us see the world a little differently. And in many cases, they help us better see ourselves.

CREATE

Animals teach us many things: how to live in the moment, what it means to be loyal, how to listen closely, why we should respect our elders. Consider what your pet has taught you. If you don't have one, think about animals you've visited at a petting park or local zoo.

Many children's books have an animal for their main character. This makes sense—children love and pay attention to what animals have to say! This week, create your own children's book character.

What animal would it be? What name would it have? What would it look like? Sketch your ideas below.

Then consider this question: What important lesson would your character teach?

We are called to care
for all living things
with the dignity and
respect with which
God cares for us.

Take Care of Teachers

Not many of you should become teachers . . . for you know that we who teach will be judged with greater strictness.

JAMES 3:1

Teachers have incredible responsibility.

This is true whether they're the ones who teach in the classroom, from the pulpit, within the home, or on the pages of the books we read. The ones who sign up to teach, especially our spiritual guides, "will be judged with greater strictness" (James 3:1).

For this reason our teachers deserve our utmost support and respect. The end of Hebrews says it well: "Obey your leaders and submit to them, for they are keeping watch over your souls, as those who will have to give an account. Let them do this with joy and not with groaning, for that would be of no advantage to you" (13:17).

In other words, if you want what's best for you, do what's best for those *over* you. Take care of your teachers.

You can do this by showing gratitude. Reach out to a teacher who has made an impact in your life by sending a card, making a call, or taking a meal. You can also do this by fulfilling the responsibilities asked of you. If you're participating in a class, read the chapter and complete the work. Don't show up unprepared week after week.

Within your congregation, honor your teachers by letting them know they can count on you. Volunteer when they need help. Offer time, money, fellowship, or support as often and in as many ways as you can.

It's especially important to honor the teachers within the home. One of the best ways we can do this is by emulating the wise and tender behaviors of our domestic teachers. Students shaped within a loving home become loving stewards in the world outside.

IMAGINE

"In paths that they have not known I will guide them. I will turn the darkness before them into light" (Isaiah 42:16). This verse refers to our ultimate Teacher, Jesus.

As you consider the gift Jesus and other teachers who walk in His footsteps are in your life, create a visual reminder with a DIY light-up jar. Simply glue gems to the outside of a jar (cover the whole thing) and glue a tea light to the inside of the jar lid. Voila. You have a lamp to carry you through dark times!

SUPPLIES:

- *Jar (any kind)*
- *Clear vase filler gems (found at any craft store)*
- *Hot glue gun*
- *Glue sticks*
- *LED tea light*

Check on Your Neighbor

For the whole law is fulfilled in one word: "You shall love your neighbor as yourself."

GALATIANS 5:14

When you're caught up in a project, caught up in life, it's easy to focus on only what *you're* doing and what *you* need. You're typing away at the computer or planning your next vacation or testing new equipment in your studio. As you're ticking off items from your checklist, are you remembering to stop every now and again to check on your neighbor?

Culture would call this the "neighborly" thing to do. A kind gesture, out of the ordinary. Scripture calls it the law.

"For the whole law is fulfilled in one word: 'You shall love your neighbor as yourself'" (Galatians 5:14). Translation? *Not optional.*

It's great that you're getting stuff done. Creative projects especially tend to make time slip by faster than we intended. We feel good. We're having fun. We're #reachinggoals and #feelingaccomplished.

But are we neglecting the bigger picture? Are we forgetting that taking moments out of our schedule to check on others–to attend to what *they're* doing and what *they* need–is more than kind? It's required. It's what sets us apart as Jesus' disciples within the world: "By this all people

As you're ticking off items from your checklist, are you remembering to stop every now and again to check on your neighbor?

will know that you are my disciples, if you have love for one another" (John 13:35).

By all means, work your checklist. But add to it: check on your neighbor.

SHARE

After being asked, "Who is my neighbor?" Jesus answered with a story about a Samaritan man who stopped to help another man who'd been robbed, beaten, and abandoned along the side of the road. The Samaritan "went to him and bound up his wounds" (Luke 10:34).

Honey is a long-known healer, used for minor wounds and burns. It's also great for chapped lips. This week, why not try making your own honey lip balm to share with your neighbor? More specific instructions can be found online, but the basics are to heat coconut oil and grated beeswax until melted; then add honey and essential oil once the mixture has cooled.

SUPPLIES:

- *Coconut oil*
- *Grated beeswax*
- *Honey*
- *Essential oil (peppermint, lavender, lemon)*
- *Small containers*

Visit Those in Need

Religion that is pure and undefiled before God the Father is this: to visit orphans and widows in their affliction.

JAMES 1:27

> In today's society the pressures of work are often the cause of neglect of our neighbor.

The laws of the Old Testament were written for an agrarian society. Thus, when teaching this society what it would look like for them to love their neighbor, the instructions had to do with their line of work:

"When you reap the harvest of your land, you shall not reap your field right up to its edge, neither shall you gather the gleanings after your harvest. You shall leave them for the poor and for the sojourner [visitor]: I am the Lord your God" (Leviticus 19:9–10).

In today's society the pressures of work are often why we neglect our neighbor, rather than the work producing bounty we draw from in order to care for them. Applying our gifts to our work is a good thing, but we must make sure that these gifts are also being stewarded in service to God and His people—especially the most vulnerable among them—as opposed to being used solely for our own ambitions.

We should ask ourselves two questions:

Are the demands of my work—whether in an office environment or on the domestic front—keeping me from serving those within my community who need real support?

How might I use my gifts to better serve those in need?

The poor. The visitor. The widow. The orphan.

These are all categories of people who still need our help today. You may not have a harvest to share, but whatever you have—goods, talents, or time—set some aside for others. However society changes, God's heart to care for the needy remains the same.

CONNECT

One of the miraculous ways God took care of His people when they were in need was sending "bread from heaven" (Exodus 16:4). Bread continues to be a staple that has carried over from ancient society to today.

As you consider the needs of others in your community—maybe you can plan a visit to a widow in a local nursing home or to a child living in a group home—try preparing a little "bread from heaven" to take along with you. You'll find dozens of easy bread recipes online. Most of the ingredients are probably in your pantry already.

Pray for Your Leaders

I urge that supplications, prayers, intercessions, and thanksgivings be made for all people, for kings and all who are in high positions.

I TIMOTHY 2:1–2

Leaders can let us down. Maybe you've experienced this on a personal level—a boss or parent or coach or pastor has disappointed you. They were supposed to be someone you could look up to; instead, they became someone you needed to forgive or, worse, hoped to forget.

The truth is leaders are people just like you and me. No matter what they're in charge of or how long they've been in that position, they're susceptible to shortcomings and errors. And often, it's the pressure they're under—the higher the position, the more pressing the demands—that leads to their mistakes.

Let's be clear: this isn't about making excuses. This is about adjusting our mindset, extending compassion, and honestly assessing: *Before I offer criticism concerning this leader, have I first offered prayers?*

As important as it is to pray for our leaders, it's also vital to make sure we're being properly led. We're all human, so mistakes are inevitable. But if prayer and discernment lead us to realize that our leaders—whether

within work, school, politics, or church—are actively pulling us away from that which is virtuous and true, it may be time to consider making a move.

REFLECT

Consider the many leaders at work in your life. Who do you appreciate, and why? What specific things have they done to support you? Help you? Teach you? Take care of you?

Choose one of those leaders and create a prayer card for him or her this week. You can write your own prayer on the leader's behalf, or you can use a scripture like Psalm 2:10–11 or Proverbs 2:1–8. Decorate the card as much as you like before mailing it. Most important, pray for this leader's work to continue thriving under his or her leadership.

SUPPLIES:

- *Card*
- *Envelope*
- *Stamp*
- *Colored pencils or markers (optional)*

Call Out to Your Father

You have received the Spirit of adoption as sons,
by whom we cry, "Abba! Father!"

ROMANS 8:15

It's an important distinction to realize God is not just your Lord; He is your Father.

In the Old Testament, the people of God knew Him as their Lord alone: "You shall love the LORD your God with all your heart and with all your soul and with all your might" (Deuteronomy 6:5).

In the New Testament, when the only begotten Son, Jesus, spoke of God, He used a different term: "I am ascending to my Father and your Father, to my God and your God" (John 20:17).

The book of Galatians says something similar: "Because you are sons, God has sent the Spirit of his Son into our hearts, crying, 'Abba! Father!'" (4:6). In Aramaic, "Abba" was the more familiar term for father, something closer to dad or daddy or papa.

In addressing God as Father, Jesus welcomes us to do the same.

In this context we understand that God's commandments are not solely issued so that we may keep His law. Rather, His commandments are issued for our own good. Just as an earthly father creates boundaries

for his children, forgives them when they falter, and loves them with both strength and tenderness, so God the Father does for us.

Isn't this amazing? That we—in humility and human fallibility—can call upon God, the Creator of the universe, the Alpha and Omega, as our *Father*. In praise, in thanksgiving, in surrender, we are invited to kneel before Him and cling to Him.

Throughout the Bible, Scripture helps us see that God is someone we can call out to, rely on, and seek comfort in. Just like we call our dads when we need them, God is available.

Call out to your Father.

IMAGINE

Rembrandt created a well-loved oil painting of the poignant father-son moment from Luke 15: *The Parable of the Prodigal Son.* Reread the story and check out the painting online. What does the painting capture of the father's emotions about his son?

Think about a father-child moment, either from this story or from your life, that you want to capture in a painting. What is it?

Why that moment? What does that moment say of a father's love? Sketch your idea below, but don't forget to make time this week to transfer your sketch onto canvas.

SUPPLIES:

- *Oil paints*
- *Palette (or wax paper)*
- *Paintbrushes*
- *Canvas*
- *Easel (optional)*

It's an important distinction to realize God is not just your Lord; He is your Father.

Feast with the Son

When he was at table with them, he took the bread
and blessed and broke it and gave it to them.

LUKE 24:30

The verse above comes from a story that took place after Jesus' crucifixion and resurrection. After startling the women at the tomb, Jesus
made Himself known to two men who "were going to a village named
Emmaus" (Luke 24:13).

What's interesting about this story is that the two men–despite
spending hours in close proximity to Jesus, walking about seven miles
with Him to Emmaus from Jerusalem–had no idea who He was. That
was, until He broke bread with them.

"He took the bread and blessed and broke it and gave it to them.
And their eyes were opened, and they recognized him" (Luke 24:30–31).

Something special happens when we feast with people. After taking
time to prepare a meal, after sitting down to eat it together, we see a side
of people they don't have the chance to show at work or on the sidewalk
or during a Sunday service. We hear their stories. We look into their eyes.
We discover who they really are.

Perhaps this is why most momentous occasions in life–whether

celebratory or somber—are marked by some kind of shared meal. In breaking bread with loved ones, new friends, or strangers, we partake in the essential acts of both offering and receiving. Slow down, sit down, share a meal, and take the time to really see the people sitting at the table with you.

PLAY

Food brings people together in a special way. This week, let the activity of cooking bring you and your loved ones together for a special purpose: to remember Christ's resurrection.

To make Resurrection Cookies, you don't need many ingredients, and you'll easily find a recipe after a quick online search. But look for one that also walks you through what each ingredient represents (for example, the vinegar reminds us of the sour wine Jesus was given to drink on the cross in Matthew 27:48). This is a great recipe for Easter—or any time you want to remember Jesus.

SUPPLIES:

- *Pecans*
- *Vinegar*
- *Egg whites*
- *Salt*
- *Sugar*

Be Fed with the Spirit

Be filled with the Spirit.

EPHESIANS 5:18

With the Spirit, there's no fear of overdoing it.

According to Matthew's gospel, after Jesus retreated in mourning over the killing of John the Baptist, the crowds followed Him on foot. Despite His heavy heart, Jesus healed the sick and went on to perform one of His most well-known miracles when he fed five thousand with just five loaves of bread and two fish. Everyone had their fill, and there was even food left over.

This was a crowd of people, sick and hungry, yet rich enough in faith to follow Jesus and stretch out their hands in hope of His healing. Just as Jesus provided for their needs with the loaves and fishes, so it is when we fill up on the Spirit–there's always enough!

So when Paul said, "And do not get drunk with wine . . . but be filled with the Spirit" (Ephesians 5:18), there's no fear of the Spirit running short. We can all take what we need, and there will still be plenty left over.

With the Spirit, there's also no fear of overdoing it.

At buffets, we tend to eat with our eyes rather than our stomachs. We pile too much on our plates and can leave feeling sick. Paul warned of this when it came to wine; getting "drunk on food" happens the same way.

But when it comes to the Spirit, we can pray as much as we want. We can sing as much as we want. We can read Scripture as much as we want. We can seek Him as much as we want "that [we] may be filled with the knowledge of his will in all spiritual wisdom and understanding" (Colossians 1:9).

There will always be enough, and no amount of His Spirit will be too much.

INSPIRE

One way to fill up on the Spirit is to sing "psalms and hymns and spiritual songs, with thankfulness in your hearts to God" (Colossians 3:16).

For this activity you have a couple of options. One is to search for an old hymnal (check thrift stores or your parents' attic) and cut out sections from hymns that you like. Glue the hymn section to a piece of folded cardstock and you have a handmade, Spirit-filled card. You can layer the hymn on top of colored paper and add ribbon for extra pizzazz.

The other option is to rewrite the lyrics to your favorite hymns on top of cardstock, decorating as much as you wish. Send your card to a friend in need of encouragement this week!

SUPPLIES:

- Hymnal (or lyrics of favorite hymn)
- Cardstock
- Glue
- Scissors
- Colored paper (optional)
- Ribbon (optional)

God Made
You for Joy

On finding joy in the little things of life,
on stopping to play, on giving thanks
and embracing today.

Today Is the Day

This is the day that the LORD has made; let us rejoice and be glad in it.

PSALM 118:24

Psalm 118 is one of the songs Jesus sang with His disciples. Part of a collection known as the "Hallel psalms," this would have been the final song they sang on the eve of His death.

"Now as they were eating, Jesus took bread, and after blessing it broke it and gave it to the disciples, and said, 'Take, eat; this is my body.' And he took a cup, and when he had given thanks he gave it to them, saying, 'Drink of it, all of you, for this is my blood'. *And when they had sung a hymn*, they went out to the Mount of Olives" (Matthew 26:26–28, 30, emphasis added).

What follows? Jesus' arrest. Peter's denial. A corrupt trial. Torture. Mockery. Betrayal from everyone He loved. Crucifixion. Separation from God the Father. And, finally, death.

Yet before all this, Jesus sang the words of Psalm 118: "This is the day that the LORD has made; let us rejoice and be glad in it" (v. 24).

It's easy to wait for another day to be joyful: when *this* is resolved . . . when *that* hasn't just fallen apart . . . when *this* isn't on the horizon. But

Jesus modeled something different.

Whatever is behind us, whatever looms ahead—today is still worth celebrating. Today is the day the Lord has made.

REFLECT

Take a few minutes to read Psalm 118 on your own. Below you'll find a selection of verses to meditate on. How do these verses apply to your life? What do they mean to you? Write your thoughts down.

Try to write specifically about whatever you're facing. Allow the words of the psalm to remind you that even though life can be difficult, you still have reasons to rejoice.

"Give thanks to the Lord, for he is good; his love endures forever." (Psalm 118:1 NIV)

"When hard pressed, I cried to the Lord; he brought me into a spacious place." (Psalm 118:5 NIV)

"The Lord is with me; I will not be afraid. What can mere mortals do to me?" (Psalm 118:6 NIV)

"It is better to take refuge in the Lord than to trust in humans." (Psalm 118:8 NIV)

"The Lord is my strength and my defense; he has become my salvation." (Psalm 118:14 NIV)

_____

_____

_____

_____

_____

_____

_____

_____

_____

_____

_____

_____

_____

_____

"This is the day
that the LORD
has made; let
us rejoice and
be glad in it."

Find Strength in Joy

Do not be grieved, for the joy of the LORD is your strength.

NEHEMIAH 8:10

Nehemiah had a specific task to fulfill. He had journeyed to Jerusalem to help the returning Israelites reclaim their city by rebuilding their wall. Without a wall, ancient peoples remained vulnerable to attack, living in fear and grief.

Hence, Nehemiah's words to the people: "Do not be grieved" (Nehemiah 8:10). And just before this: "This day is holy to the LORD your God; do not mourn or weep" (v. 9). These were not words of comfort absent from action. Nehemiah's address came with instruction: "Do not be grieved, *for the joy of the* LORD *is your strength*" (v. 10, emphasis added).

Trials and tribulations are inevitable, but their existence does not negate seasons of abundance and celebration. Suffering and joy can indeed exist in close proximity–often at the same time. We're assured that even in the midst of our seasons of suffering (and there definitely will be seasons . . . several of them!), we should draw our strength to get through them from God. In turning toward Him–even in the bad times– we're able to find the energy and the healing we need to get through.

> Suffering and joy can indeed exist in close proximity—often at the same time.

It is not in grief or even anger where we find our true strength, but it is found in *joy*. The miraculous and infinite joy that is rooted in the Lord is the greatest strength of all.

There's "a time to mourn," Ecclesiastes 3:4 reminds us, but right after this, we're told there's a time to dance, to celebrate. A time for joy.

It's in this response–specifically the joy *of the Lord*–that we find the strength we need to keep going. To fulfill *our* task. To rebuild whatever spiritual walls we've let come down, so we're no longer living in fear.

PLAY

There's "a time to mourn, and a time to dance" (Ecclesiastes 3:4). Let's make today your time to dance! Not because everything in life is going great. Not because every situation or circumstance or relationship or responsibility makes you happy. But because God is good, and this never changes! No matter what, our joy *in the Lord* can be stable.

Find a pocket of time this week or weekend to play your favorite worship songs and dance. Move the chairs in the living room. Turn up the music. Get the whole family involved. There are no rules, just joy. Go ahead, dance like no one's watching.

Become Like a Child

"Truly, I say to you, unless you turn and become like children, you will never enter the kingdom of heaven."

MATTHEW 18:3

Usually, when we read this verse, we think of a child's trust and dependence. They believe what they are told and lean on the ones leading them.

But if you've been around a child lately, you've probably noticed they are much more than dependent: they are also silly and imaginative and unaware of social norms. They'll wear socks that don't match and a hoodie inside out. They'll talk to themselves and make up words, and find hours of enjoyment from a backyard of trees and a walking stick.

Children know how to make the most of every moment. They laugh— often. They prioritize play.

When we become adults, however, our priorities change. We wear clothes that match and care more about what others think of us than the things we want to try, the opportunities before us, or a moment's worth of fun. We start seeing playtime as a waste of time, valuing productivity over pretending.

It's true. Priorities change as responsibilities mount, and being productive is a good thing. But don't forget where you began: it's okay to laugh. (Ecclesiastes 3:4 says there's time for that.) It's *good* to play. Your spirit will thank you if you take a step back from stress today and find a moment to have fun.

EXPLORE

Outside of Scripture encouraging us to "become like children," modern research has proven the benefits of playtime for adults: it reduces stress, stimulates brain function (including creativity), and boosts your energy. *Sign me up!*

So here is your task for the week: become like a child.

Think of the things you loved doing when you were growing up. Swinging from the monkey bars, kicking a soccer ball, swimming in a sun-warmed lake, and feeling the mud squish around your toes. Maybe you enjoyed painting with no plan in mind, or creating a new invention from fresh, malleable clay. Wherever you found joy in your younger years, go there.

If you have small children, use this as an opportunity to play alongside them. Join them in one of their favorite activities, or introduce them to one of your own childhood pastimes.

Feel the stress melt away as you make time for play.

Look at the Birds

"Look at the birds of the air: they neither sow nor reap nor gather into barns, and yet your heavenly Father feeds them."

MATTHEW 6:26

Jesus taught His disciples to "look at the birds of the air," thereby discerning the Father's care for them. For if the Father cared so tenderly for something as simple as a sparrow (worth pennies in Jesus' day), would He not care even more for His chosen people?

Surely Jesus knew when He suggested this pastime that birdwatching has benefits not only for the soul but also for the body and mind. In fact, a recent research study conducted by the University of Exeter found that watching birds has positive effects such as decreasing stress, lowering risk of depression, and reducing anxiety.[1] Some doctors are now even prescribing activities like park visits to their patients.

Between hectic morning routines and traffic jams and the endless

> If the Father cared
> so tenderly for
> something as simple
> as a sparrow . . .
> would He not care
> even more for His
> chosen people?

to-do lists, it's easy to get caught up in daily stresses here on the ground. But what if we looked up?

Today, turn your eyes to the sky, where you might find a few birds fluttering among the sunlit clouds or the moon's early evening glow. Watch as they float through the air, coasting on the wind in a graceful and instinctual dance. Let this inspire you to adapt a similar mindset as you move through the day. Take note of the winds around you and tune your decisions to their rhythms.

Jesus knew what we would need because He took part in creating us: "For by him all things were created, in heaven and on earth. All things were created through him and for him" (Colossians 1:16). And our Creator prescribed us to "look at the birds of the air." We might add "take a walk in the woods" or "watch the sunset" or "spend the morning on a beach."

Wherever you live, you have the gift of the outdoors around you. Protect your mental health and soak it in!

CONNECT

To watch birds, you first need to attract them. This week's activity is to create a simple, yet adorable, bird feeder for your backyard or garden.

A teacup bird feeder (instructions online) is one of many options for this DIY project. If you don't have an old teacup and saucer lying around, just waiting to be repurposed, try creating a bird feeder out of a cleaned-out grapefruit or, even simpler, pine cones. Most of what you need is right at home!

SUPPLIES:

- *Old teacup and saucer*
- *Ceramic glue*
- *Twine*
- *Birdseed*
- *Bird feeder hanger (optional)*

Stay Focused on Today

"Do not be anxious about tomorrow. Sufficient for the day is its own trouble."

MATTHEW 6:34

Life is unpredictable. No matter what kind of effort we put in, things can still fall apart.

Because so many facets of life are outside of our control, we worry. It's not that we're trying to "invent disaster" by worrying it into existence; we've simply experienced it before. We've been burned by the unprecedented health crisis, the unimagined divorce, the unpredictable firing pattern of a company.

Our mind jumps to conclusions, burdening today with tomorrow's imagined worry.

Jesus, knowing this, gave us a gentle reminder: "Therefore do not be anxious about tomorrow, for tomorrow will be anxious for itself. Sufficient for the day is its own trouble" (Matthew 6:34).

Life is hard. You're not wrong if you think you might be burned again. But even so, Jesus is saying this: do yourself a favor and don't try to face every mountain every day. Face *today's* mountain. And spare yourself the energy it takes to be anxious about tomorrow.

If you back up a few verses in Matthew 6, you'll realize that Jesus' preference is that we'd not even be anxious for today (v. 25). How is that possible? Jesus taught us to remember the Father's loving care (v. 26), and Paul taught us to face each day's hurdles and unwanted surprises with prayer (Philippians 4:6).

GROW

This week, set aside about half an hour, find a quiet place, and write down whatever is causing you to feel anxious. Projects? Deadlines? Relationships? Responsibilities? Unmet needs or expectations? You can write a list or write a letter to your loving Father.

Once you have a clearer idea of what's on your heart, create a worry jar for your current fears. You just need any empty jar and slips of paper. You can decorate your jar; one suggestion is to attach a sticker on the outside of the jar with Matthew 6:26 or Philippians 4:6 written on it. Then, for as many days as it takes, write each worry, one by one, on a piece of paper. After praying about it, drop it in the jar. Take it one day, one worry at a time, and repeat until they're all in the jar.

SUPPLIES:

- *Mason jar*
- *Blank sticker (optional)*
- *Paper*

Embrace the Gift

Come, see a man who told me all that I ever did.
Can this be the Christ?

JOHN 4:29

Though the Jews and Samaritans had many dividing lines, waiting for the Messiah was not one of them. So when this Samaritan woman was confronted by someone who knew intimate details of her past, even before she'd shared her name, she asked, "Can this be the Christ?"

This man was strange. Special. Unique. Could He be the One her people had been waiting for?

Scripture says that after this encounter, she "left her water jar and went away into town and said to the people, 'Come, see a man who told me all that I ever did . . .'" (John 4:28–29). The reason she came to the well was irrelevant after encountering Jesus–something more important had happened. She attended to the mystery, to the marvel, to the miracle of this moment immediately.

Albert Einstein is attributed as saying, "Coincidence is God's way of remaining anonymous." It's true—strange things happen, and we forget to take notice.

Instead, embrace the gift of the moment. When the divine collides with your seemingly ordinary day, put down whatever you're in the middle of and share with your town, your friends, and your family what He has done.

SHARE

What coincidences have you let slide that might have been God at work? Consider those moments when things just came together, maybe even at the last minute. Consider the times when you didn't think you'd finish a task and then it all fell into place. Consider the people who came into your life at just the right time.

God is good, isn't He?

Today, share at least one of your experiences with someone who might still be young in their faith. To find this person, ask your church's youth minister, if you have one, or talk to a parent of a teenager within your congregation. Seek the name of a young person with whom you can write a letter and share your good news about God.

SUPPLIES:

- *Paper*
- *Envelope*
- *Stamp*

Take Your Break

There is nothing better for a person than that he should eat and drink and find enjoyment in his toil.

ECCLESIASTES 2:24

Life gets complicated. Schedules are jam-packed with activities, literally from sunup to sundown some days. Your lunch hour–instead of a time to stop, relax, and savor–becomes another few minutes when you can finish a task, make a phone call, read an email.

In Ecclesiastes, the writer was speaking from the other side of those experiences. He'd lived a full life, trying just about everything we could imagine. He'd been a gardener, an architect, a business owner, a collector, a bookworm, a lover, a partier, and a king. Yet, at the end of it all, he said: "There is nothing better for a person than that he should eat and drink and find enjoyment in his toil. This also, I saw, is from the hand of God, for apart from him who can eat or who can have enjoyment?" (Ecclesiastes 2:24–25).

It's not that your life shouldn't be full, but be careful it doesn't sweep you away–don't keep pushing, going, doing, trying if it means losing sight of what matters most.

When life demands much of you, set some boundaries, beginning

> It's not that your life shouldn't be full, but be careful it doesn't sweep you away.

with taking that lunch break. Use times like those to silence your phone, leave your computer, and get back to what matters most: a meal with your family, sipping coffee with a friend, completing a task you enjoy.

RELAX

When it's been an especially trying week, listen to the needs of your body and find pockets of time when you can step away from work and be still. Sometimes the silence and stillness are enough to rejuvenate you—body, mind, and soul—for the demands of the next day.

To prep for those times, create your own lavender bath salt this week (search online for instructions). The process is incredibly simple. You only need a couple of ingredients, but you can add optional things like pink Himalayan sea salt for color or dried lavender flowers. If you know a friend who could use a gentle reminder to take a break, share some of your mix with them!

SUPPLIES:
- *Jar*
- *Epsom salt*
- *Lavender essential oil*

Keep Dancing

"The LORD chose me. So I will continue dancing and celebrating in front of the LORD."

2 SAMUEL 6:21 ERV

If you're doing something creative, taking a chance, and stepping out in faith, critics will come. They might make fun of you, as Michal did to her husband, King David, in 2 Samuel. He had been dancing and leaping and offering praise before the Lord–and before the eyes of all the people–when she said: "How the king of Israel honored himself today, uncovering himself today before the eyes of his servants' female servants, as one of the vulgar fellows shamelessly uncovers himself!" (2 Samuel 6:20).

His response? "It was before the LORD, who chose me. And I will celebrate before the LORD" (v. 21). In other words, *I'm not doing this for you. I'm doing this for Him. His approval alone is good enough for me.*

You will face critics too. They might doubt you, questioning your judgment

> **If you're doing something creative, taking a chance, and stepping out in faith, critics will come.**

and misinterpreting your motives. They might make fun of you, put you down, tell you to quit. Maybe you're facing the world's worst critic right now: yourself. Maybe you're hearing these words inside your own head.

Remember what Theodore Roosevelt said: "It is not the critic who counts. . . . The credit belongs to the man who is actually in the arena." So keep dancing, praising, trying, writing, making, doing. God's approval is enough.

IMAGINE

In a psalm of thanksgiving, David wrote: "Weeping may tarry for the night, but joy comes with the morning. . . . You have turned for me my mourning into dancing; you have loosed my sackcloth and clothed me with gladness" (Psalm 30:5, 11).

What does joy look like to you? Is it a child dancing? A blooming flower? A father smiling at his son? Think about your most joy-filled moments and sketch one of them below. Then choose one colored pencil—the one that most captures the color of joy to you—and add spots of color to your sketch.

SUPPLIES:

- *Pencil*
- *Colored pencil*

Split the Earth

All the people went up after him, playing on pipes,
and rejoicing with great joy, so that the earth was
split by their noise.

1 KINGS 1:40

Toward the end of David's life, he granted permission for his son Solomon to be anointed Israel's next king. "So Zadok the priest . . . went down and had Solomon ride on King David's mule. There Zadok the priest took the horn of oil from the tent and anointed Solomon" (1 Kings 1:38–39). What followed was a celebration so loud "that the earth was split by their noise" (v. 40).

Some moments are worth celebrating–and in a big way! Some moments are worth "splitting the earth" with your joy, your music, your good-time rabble of close friends and family who support you through life's most treasured moments.

When you graduate. When you marry. When you're awaiting your first child. Those are celebratory moments for sure. But what about . . . when you launch your online shop? When you finish your first book? When you complete a year of recovery?

Don't let important milestones slip away unnoticed. Go big, get

out the pipes and tambourines, and celebrate life's greatest moments, remembering to give thanks to the One who helped you along the way. For nothing is impossible with Him (Luke 1:37), but also, what is possible without Him?

CONNECT

Invite a group of friends over for a night of split-the-earth merriment, music, and joy. An easy way to do this is to borrow a few hymnals from your church building and make this a night of a cappella praise and worship. But if you have friends who play instruments, ask if they can bring them along!

Another option—if you really want to go for it—is to rent a karaoke machine. Gather some friends for a night of all-star living room performances. Remember, the important thing is not how good you sound but how your hearts are centered on thanking God for all of the treasured moments in your lives.

SUPPLIES:

- *Hymnals*
- *Instruments (optional)*

Some moments are worth celebrating— and in a big way!

Delight in His Care

My soul shall exult in my God, for he has clothed me with the garments of salvation.

ISAIAH 61:10

The word *exult* is another way of saying rejoice, be joyful, take delight in. In this verse, the writer was taking delight in the lavishness of God's care:

"I will sing for joy in GOD, explode in praise from deep in my soul! He dressed me up in a suit of salvation, he outfitted me in a robe of righteousness, as a bridegroom who puts on a tuxedo and a bride a jeweled tiara. So the Master, GOD, brings righteousness into full bloom and puts praise on display before the nations" (Isaiah 61:10-11 MSG).

From rags to riches. From dry desert to blooms. This is the story of every disciple of Christ. Despite our mistakes, despite our weaknesses, despite the moments when we wonder whether we're good enough or ever will be, we are bedecked with the beauty of righteousness.

Covered, adorned, lavished with His care.

So Isaiah exulted: What else can we do? We don't deserve

From dry desert to blooms. This is the story of every disciple of Christ.

this. We haven't earned the right to have His help and attention. But He gives it nonetheless. And the truth is, He doesn't only provide just what we need to survive. He looks to us and asks, "How can I make their lives beautiful?"

What He gives is far beyond what we need to make it through.

INSPIRE

What better season to remember the lavishness of God's love than Christmastime? The gift of Jesus to the world far surpasses any other gift God has provided (John 3:16).

To prep for Christmas, try making your own bejeweled orna-ments. All you need is ordinary Christmas balls (any size, any color) and a package of your favorite inexpensive jewels. Hot glue the jewels to the outside of the ball, taking your Christmas decor from ordinary to extraordinary. Let this process remind you of the time and attention God takes to elevate your life in a similar way.

SUPPLIES:

- *Christmas ball(s)*
- *Plastic jewels*
- *Hot glue gun*

Take Time to Rest

By God's will I may come to you with joy and be refreshed in your company.

ROMANS 15:32

Paul made it to Rome, but not in the way he expected. When he arrived, he was under arrest, and any friends he was hoping to refresh with his company would have had to change their expectations. They could see him, but only if they paid him a visit . . . in prison.

Life doesn't always go the way we plan. We're looking forward to a vacation, only to have it canceled at the last minute. We're excited to meet up with friends for dinner, only to learn they're not feeling well and need to reschedule. Bigger disappoints come, too, of course. Life has unexpected twists around nearly every corner.

Because of this, it's important that we do what we can to refresh each other. Another translation of Romans 15:32 says it this way: "I will come with joy, and together you and I will have a time of rest" (ERV).

Just as Paul and his friends had to face an unexpected turn of events, our "times of rest" are sometimes forced upon us by circumstance, the conditions of which aren't always ideal. But when we find ourselves in situations we never would have foreseen, we have an opportunity to

discover new ways we can rest and refresh together, finding moments of stillness and recovery in the midst of life's unexpected messes. If a friend cancels dinner at the last minute, take the evening to call a distant relative you've been meaning to reach out to. If your vacation plans fall through, how about an impromptu road trip or a relaxing staycation instead? Learning how to pivot and still find spiritual refreshment during these small hiccups will prepare us to deal with larger challenges down the road. If and when tragedy strikes, we'll be able to take it in stride and treat it as an opportunity to show up for one another.

After all, when we help one another find refreshment in the unexpected, we'll find that God is there with us as well.

SHARE

Do you know a friend, family member, coworker, or neighbor who's navigating a particularly disappointing season right now? A simple thing you can do to bring a little joy into their life is delivering a bouquet of flowers.

You can always purchase a ready-made bouquet, but for an extra-special touch, try making your own. You'll find all the materials you need at a craft store. Then cut flowers from your garden or pick them up from a florist. As you trim and assemble, pray for your friend—ask God to help them cling to hope even as they face a difficult season.

SUPPLIES:
- *Flowers*
- *Scissors*
- *Floral tape*
- *Decorative ribbon (optional)*

It's important
that we do what
we can to refresh
each other.

Treasure at Your Fingertips

Your laws are my treasure; they are my heart's delight.

PSALM 119:111 NLT

We often think of treasure as hard to come by, as something extravagant. When the stack of monthly bills grows taller, when the kids outgrow yet another pair of shoes, the images of wealth and glamour we see on television and social media seem like a world away. Yet the Bible says, "Your laws are my treasure; they are my heart's delight" (Psalm 119:111 NLT). Maybe treasure isn't so hard to come by after all.

Maybe treasure is what we find when we spend an evening with our family, playing shadow puppets on the ceiling, making memories that will last forever. Maybe treasure is the feeling of the warm sun on our skin, or the flutter of a fall breeze in our hair. Maybe treasure is what we stumble upon when we invest in friendships with people who support and help and nurture us, through good times and bad.

Treasure is what we encounter every time we open God's Word. It's at our fingertips, every hour of every day.

While worldly material goods will one day succumb to ruin, God's treasures are infinite. We're told in Matthew 6:19–21, "Do not lay up for yourselves treasures on earth, where moth and rust destroy and where thieves break in and steal, but lay up for yourselves treasures in heaven. For where your treasure is, there your heart will be also."

The treasure of Jesus' love is extravagant and endless, regardless of how many people open their hearts to it. The Bible is one place you can encounter that love every day. The more you indulge in it, the more you will have to share. Don't let your treasure slip by unnoticed—you have a gem within your hands.

REFLECT

One way to encourage yourself to treasure those things we tend to take for granted, like God's Word, is to create your own Scripture signs. By turning your favorite verses into artwork, you'll have visual cues to remind you what gems those words really are.

A simple option for this is to purchase chalkboard spray paint and repurpose a piece of particle board. Once finished, attach a piece of twine so you can hang your sign, or create a wooden frame to go around it. The best part is you can change out the verse daily or weekly—a great reminder that the Bible is full of valuable words just waiting to be taken in.

SUPPLIES:

- *Particle board*
- *Chalkboard spray paint*
- *Chalkboard markers*
- *Twine*
- *Wood for frame (optional)*
- *Paint or stain for frame (optional)*

Take Joy

A joyful heart is good medicine, but a crushed spirit dries up the bones.

PROVERBS 17:22

God made you for joy.

If you're in the midst of a challenging season of life, or even one where you feel as if you're just coasting by, this may be a tough truth to believe. It's understandably difficult to look at the conditions of our earthly existence and find it full of joy. Life is often brimming with confusion, heartache, and pain. But we don't find joy by looking to this world to supply it. We discover joy by understanding that it comes from God, who created this world and every living thing in it.

God, and His goodness, are constant. Hebrews 13:8 says, "Jesus Christ is the same yesterday and today and forever." So, too, are the goodness and mercy and loving-kindness He brings into our lives: yesterday, today, forever.

So whatever happens today, we are still made for joy. It's this assurance of our identity that allows us—in all seasons—to live with joy that is not dependent on circumstance. Even when it's tough for us to find it, that joy is always there for us. Yesterday, today, forever.

Joy is the antidote to life's suffering. Said another way, joy is not found in taking something; joy is what we take to combat life's loneliness and fatigue and heartache and pain. Joy is what we choose.

CREATE

Just like there's science behind the benefits of joy, there's science behind the healing power of chicken noodle soup. The vegetables promote immune system recovery, the broth hydrates you and opens your airways, and the chicken provides much-needed protein while your body is working hard to fight antigens.

Search online until you find a recipe you want to try, and then make your own pot of chicken noodle soup to share with your family. This is a great weeknight meal, even if you're feeling well. As you savor the comforting broth, remember to also savor life's joy-filled moments: yesterday, today, forever.

SUPPLIES:

- *Chicken broth*
- *Vegetables (carrots, celery, onion)*
- *Chicken*
- *Noodles*
- *Herbs*

God, and His goodness, are constant.

God Made You for Growth

On trying new things, on developing your talents, on leaning on God and learning about yourself in the process of growth.

You Are Being Led

We are his workmanship, created in Christ Jesus
for good works, which God prepared beforehand,
that we should walk in them.

EPHESIANS 2:10

In John 10, Jesus gives us a metaphor of how He interacts with His
people: "He who enters by the door is the shepherd of the sheep . . . The
sheep hear his voice, and he calls his own sheep by name and leads them
out . . . He goes before them, and the sheep follow him, for they know
his voice" (John 10:2–4).

Jesus sees you. Jesus knows you. Jesus calls you by name and leads
you along the way.

These are words to remember when life feels random, chaotic, scat-
tered like sheep roaming aimlessly on a hill without a shepherd. *Does my
work matter? Am I doing what I should be doing? Am I wasting time on this?
Am I wandering down the wrong way?*

Whatever you are invested in, no matter how fruitless the work seems
to be, Jesus is there with you.

Why? Because you are His workmanship. Do you remember this
verse? *You are His masterpiece.* He created you for something beyond

what you could imagine for yourself. And He isn't leaving you to figure that plan out for yourself; He's leading you so you can live out the plan with Him.

> **Jesus sees you. Jesus knows you.**

If it seems that things aren't working, no matter how many different avenues you've tried, bring this to Jesus. Ask Him to guide you with discernment; ask Him to whisper to you so you can hear His gentle call. Is there a chance that you've gone off course? Have you been following your own path instead of the one He paved before you? Like a sheep to the shepherd, listen for the call of Jesus as He leads you toward the lighted way.

EXPLORE

To remind yourself that you are not wandering—*you are being led*—why not repurpose one of those old maps or atlases you're not using anymore? An easy project is decoupaging a blank canvas with a map of the city where you live or, perhaps, the city where you'd like to live one day. You'll find more detailed instructions online, but the essential supply list is included here.

Once you're done attaching the map to your canvas, use the Sharpie to add whatever message, quote, or Scripture you'd like on the front. One suggestion is Proverbs 3:5–6: "Trust in the LORD with all your heart . . . and he will make straight your paths."

SUPPLIES:

- Canvas (any size)
- Map
- Paintbrush
- Mod Podge (a glue, sealer, and finish)
- Sharpie
- Scissors

Watch How You Walk

Walk in a manner worthy of the Lord, fully
pleasing to him: bearing fruit in every good work.

COLOSSIANS 1:10

To try something new—something that
requires an investment of your time, talents,
and resources without a guarantee of how it
will turn out—is a step of faith. You're taking
a great risk, and you're trusting God to be
leading you along the journey.

> To try
> something
> new . . . is a
> step of faith.

But somewhere after those first steps, our
focus begins to drift. We start to question where we are going, and
whether we should be going another way and whether this might be a
dead end. Basically, we want to know: What if I fail?

What's interesting about Colossians 1:10 is it doesn't talk about the
road we're walking at all. Instead, it focuses on *how* we're walking: "Walk
in a manner worthy of the Lord, fully pleasing to him: bearing fruit in
every good work and increasing in the knowledge of God."

Other scriptures contribute to this idea: "You make known to me the
path of life" . . . "He leads me in paths of righteousness for his name's

sake" . . . "You search out my path and my lying down and are acquainted with all my ways" (Psalm 16:11; 23:3; 139:3).

In other words, the business of which road we take is God's to handle. Our business is to focus on how we're walking, allowing every investment of time, effort, and resources to bear fruit for His glory and bring honor to His name.

REFLECT

Use the poem template below to help you visualize the walk you're on with Jesus. Fill in the blanks with word pictures of how He makes you feel. You can add stanzas to the poem if you want; make it your own, and let the words you write grow your trust in His ability to guide you.

Lord, I am a sheep; You are my Shepherd.

When I walk with You, I feel safe.

You care for me like _____.

Lord, I am a child; You are my Father.

When I follow Your lead, I have no fears.

You protect me like _____.

Lord, I am clay; You are the Potter.

When I am shaped by You, I become a masterpiece.

You love me like _____.

Don't Look Back

When the grass is gone . . . new growth appears
and the vegetation of the mountains is gathered.

PROVERBS 27:25

You cannot
experience new
growth until you're
willing to leave
the old behind.

To give time and attention to some new endeavor inevitably means taking time and attention away from something else. We can't just keep adding more tasks to our day . . . we only have so much time, and our energy runs short.

So Proverbs advises, "Cut the hay, and new grass will grow" (27:25 ERV). Easier said than done, perhaps. *Cut the hay* might mean letting go of something important to you. *Cut the hay* might mean leaving behind something you've invested a lot of time in.

But you cannot experience new growth until you're willing to leave the old behind.

In the Gospel of Luke, a hopeful but naive disciple told Jesus, "I will follow you, Lord," followed quickly by, "but let me first say farewell to those at my home." Jesus responded, "No one who puts his hand to the plow and looks back is fit for the kingdom of God" (9:61–62).

Don't look back. This is not how we say yes. This is not how we try the new thing. This is not how we grow or finally find success, blooming somewhere amidst the hundreds of times we might have failed.

Only when the grass is gone does new growth appear.

IMAGINE

Everyone from Claude Monet to Georgia O'Keeffe to Andy Warhol has been inspired by blooms. You can find hundreds of famous paintings with fields of flowers, in nearly every style.

Try your own abstract painting of a favorite flower (search O'Keeffe's work for examples). When you finish, find a spot where you can hang it as a reminder of your bloom to come. You may have to wait for it. You may have to let go of something else you've enjoyed and spent time on and cared for. But focus on what's ahead and celebrate the beauty of new growth!

SUPPLIES:

- *Acrylic paints*
- *Palette (or wax paper)*
- *Paintbrushes*
- *Canvas or paper*
- *Rag (or paper towels)*
- *Cup of water*
- *Varnish*
- *Easel (optional)*

Growth Takes Time

We count as blessed those who have persevered.

JAMES 5:11 NIV

The hardest part of any project isn't getting started. In the early days your excitement carries you through. But somewhere after the first few days or weeks or months, your energy begins to wane.

The hardest part is getting through to the end.

When what was new and teeming with excitement becomes mundane, part of the routine, it's easy to forget why you started.

Or maybe it's not that your project becomes mundane, but it doesn't seem to be going anywhere. You're not sure why you should carry on, because what's the point? The investment of time and energy isn't worth it when it's not yielding results.

"Be patient," James would say. "See how the farmer waits for the precious fruit of the earth, being patient about it, until it receives the early and the late rains. . . . Behold, we consider those

> "We consider those blessed who remained steadfast" (James 5:11).

blessed who remained steadfast" (James 5:7, 11).

The blessed are not the beginners, according to James. The blessed are those who see things through to the end. Those who don't quit when things get hard, when energy is hard to come by, when the results remain yet still hidden.

Be patient. Growth takes time.

PLAY

If you want an activity that will help grow your patience, brush the dust off of that one-thousand-piece puzzle your grandmother bought you several years ago. Or you can step up the creativity a notch and try creating your own.

Take a purposeful walk around your neighborhood or in a nearby park, and snap a photo of something you find beautiful. Then turn that memory into an even more lasting experience by utilizing an online photo service to create a puzzle. Whether with your family, with friends, or on your own, take an evening to put aside the electronics and revisit that special memory, piece by piece.

One Task for Today

We all . . . are being transformed into the same image from one degree of glory to another.

2 CORINTHIANS 3:18

A well-known proverb asks, "How do you eat an elephant?" The response is, "One bite at a time."

There aren't many (*any?*) scenarios when we would need to eat an elephant, but the lesson stands. How do we accomplish anything that seems larger than life, that seems beyond-us impossible?

One day, one task, one moment of obedience at a time.

This is the only way to see your project through to the end. You need only manage your bite-size chunk today. What one contribution can you make? What fifteen minutes of work can you accomplish? What brushstroke can you add? What helper can you call?

Focus on the one task for today; the rest will fall into place.

What's comforting and fascinating and encouraging is that while you are doing your one task, walking the path God has laid out for you, God is doing His one task on you, shaping and transforming you to reflect His glory (2 Corinthians 3:18). Even God takes it slow, one day and one change and one degree of glory at a time.

Eventually, the master-
piece comes into view.

PLAN

A great way to stay on track with your project is to set a SMART goal for yourself. That means your goal is specific, measurable, achievable, relevant, and timebound. A simple example would be "I want to finish writing the first draft of my book by the end of the year."

SMART goals can help you see the endgame goal so you can work your way back to today. What one contribution can you make today toward your larger goal? Example: "I will write for thirty minutes each weekday morning for the next month."

Create your daily task today, write it on a Post-it Note, and stick it on a place where you'll see it each day. Take it one day at a time to reach your goal!

SUPPLIES:
- *Post-it Notes*

You Can

"I will be with you."

EXODUS 3:12

Moses was minding his own business, tending to sheep and loving his family. He grew up in the palace of Egypt, but as a young adult, he fled after standing up for the people of his heritage rather than standing with the people of his home.

But it was time.

"The LORD said, 'I have surely seen the affliction of my people who are in Egypt . . . and I have come down to deliver them out of the hand of the Egyptians'" (Exodus 3:7–8). Then, He revealed why He said these things to Moses: "Come, I will send *you* . . . that you may bring my people, the children of Israel, out of Egypt" (v. 10, emphasis added).

Why me? How can I do this? Will it work out?

If you're asking questions like these of your situation, you'll appreciate Moses' story. His response to the Lord's calling: "Who am I?" (v. 11).

I'm not impressive. I don't have a résumé like hers. I'm not as talented as he is. I don't know how to manage it all. I'll probably mess this up.

Whatever your list of reasons why you shouldn't take the risk and try the thing God has placed on your heart, you're not alone. Every other person in the arena of achieving life's dreams has dealt with the same emotions and asked similar questions.

The reason *you can*, just like Moses, is simple: the Lord will be with you.

CREATE

When the Lord met Moses in Exodus 3, it was on a mountain in the midst of a burning bush. This was the well-known moment when God said, "Do not come near; take your sandals off your feet, for the place on which you are standing is holy ground" (v. 5).

God often met His people in the form of fire in the Old Testament. As a nod to that, and a way to remember that God's flame burns inside you (2 Timothy 1:6), try creating your own candle this week (the internet has several how-tos). Add some calming essential oils like lavender to the wax so you can burn your handmade craft, take a deep breath, and be reminded that you are not alone.

SUPPLIES:

- *Wax*
- *Wick*
- *Container*
- *Fragrance (optional)*
- *Popsicle sticks*

Nothing Is Wasted

He said to them, "Follow me, and I will make you fishers of men."

MATTHEW 4:19

Maybe you're not being called to something new altogether. Maybe you're being asked to pivot—to take an old skill and apply it in a new way. Consider the disciples, for example: "While walking by the Sea of Galilee, he saw two brothers, Simon (who is called Peter) and Andrew his brother, casting a net into the sea, for they were fishermen. And he said to them, 'Follow me, and I will make you fishers of men'" (Matthew 4:18–19).

These men didn't leave the skills and know-how of their experience behind; they changed how, and where, and among whom they applied it.

What do you do well?

What do you already know?

In what are you experienced?

When you move on to a new venture, it can seem like everything behind you is wasted. *Why did I train for so long? Why did I work to master that skill, especially if one day I'd just leave it all behind?*

Nothing is wasted. God chose you "before the foundation of the world, that [you] should be holy and blameless before him" (Ephesians

> Maybe you're not being called to something new altogether. Maybe you're being asked to pivot.

1:4). Whatever you've learned, however you've grown, whomever you've met, don't imagine you're throwing it away.

Apply *everything* about you to what's ahead.

GROW

Want a visual representation of what it means not to throw something out, but to give it new purpose? Stop throwing out your plastic milk jugs, juice containers, and one- or two-liter bottles. After you have a small collection (maybe five or six), then convert your would-be trash into a small indoor or outdoor herb garden.

You will find several renditions of this online; explore the options and find a creative solution that works best for your collection of plastic bottles. Remember, nothing need be wasted!

SUPPLIES:

- *Plastic bottles (any size, any kind)*
- *Herb seedlings*
- *Potting soil*
- *Scissors*
- *Craft knife*
- *Sharpie*

Stop Comparing

When Peter saw him, he said to Jesus, "Lord, what about this man?"

JOHN 21:21

If someone serves in a different capacity. . . what is that to you?

You know good people. The woman at your church who cooks lunch for the homeless every Thursday. You know talented people. The teenager who made an album before he was fifteen and now has a record deal. You know brave people. The veteran who took a chance on a small business idea.

Then there's the seemingly ordinary you.

Whatever you do, it's easy to feel that other people's work is more important. Whatever you've accomplished, haven't others accomplished more? Yet you, too, are good and talented and brave.

When Peter started comparing himself to the disciples around him, Jesus answered, "If it is my will that he remain until I come, what is that to you? You follow me!" (John 21:22).

If someone serves in a different capacity, if someone accomplishes something at a different pace, if someone takes a different chance, what is that to you? The work of others doesn't in any way diminish the work planned for you.

We're reminded in Romans 12:4–6 NIV, "For just as each of us has one body with many members, and these members do not all have the same function, so in Christ we, though many, form one body, and each member belongs to all the others. We have different gifts, according to the grace given to each of us."

So, stop comparing, and start celebrating. Whether we eat or drink, whatever we do, let's do it all to the glory of God (1 Corinthians 10:31).

CONNECT

Let's be honest. The work of others, especially in a field where we're hoping to "get our shot," can make us jealous. We want the success someone else is experiencing.

This week, choose to celebrate someone else's success instead of dismissing it, downplaying it, or wishing it was yours. Is there a musician you respect? An artist, writer, actor, quilter, or designer whose work inspires you? Visit their website so you can find a mailing address. Then, write them a letter! Let them know how thankful you are for their contribution to the world.

Better yet, is there someone within your own community who is working hard to accomplish great success? Perhaps you'd like to write them a note as well. We must remember that even the people in our lives who seem to have it all are likely dealing with many of the same insecurities that cause us to doubt ourselves.

SUPPLIES:

- *Paper*
- *Envelope*
- *Stamp*

Stop Seeking Signs

For Jews demand signs and Greeks seek wisdom,
but we preach Christ crucified.

1 CORINTHIANS 1:22–23

Taking your shot often involves risk. It requires investment. Waves of doubt may suddenly overtake you: *Can I do this? Should I do this? What if I lose everything? How will it work out?*

Gideon likely asked similar questions when God called on him to raise an army against the oppressive Midianites (Judges 6–7). Talk about doing the impossible. Gideon–a non-warrior, non-bodybuilder, normal guy–was tasked with leading an army of three hundred against one hundred *thousand*–plus.

So Gideon asked for a sign.

The Jews of the New Testament did the same. When it came to believing that a man who seemed by all accounts normal was actually the Warrior-King Messiah upon whom Israel had been waiting for four hundred–plus years, "they asked him to show them a sign from heaven" (Matthew 16:1).

Jesus didn't always shun their lack of belief. Many times He offered just what they asked for: visible proof of His godship in a miracle feeding, for instance, or in the raising of a man from the dead. God responded to Gideon similarly, providing fire and dew and other concrete reasons to believe in Him.

The problem isn't wanting proof; the problem is having proof and still not believing, having proof and continually seeking more. At some point it comes down to trust: knowing God loves you, and that He knows what's best for you and is leading you toward it. Can you trust Him enough to stop seeking signs and just listen? Be still, be quiet, and wait to hear His whisper.

REFLECT

One of Gideon's problems—one of the reasons he couldn't accept God's plan for him without signs—was how he saw himself. God's angel appeared to him and said, "The LORD is with you, O mighty man of valor" (Judges 6:12). But Gideon responded, "Behold, my clan is the weakest in Manasseh, and I am the least in my father's house" (v. 15).

How do you see yourself? Try creating your own self-portrait in pencil this week. Position a mirror so you can see yourself as you draw; highlight your best features, especially those that make you unique. Give thanks for all the good things you see in yourself as you sketch.

SUPPLIES:

- *Graphite pencil*
- *Eraser*
- *Kneaded eraser (optional)*

- *Pencil sharpener*
- *Sketch pad or mat board*

Face the Lack

"With man this is impossible, but with God all things are possible."

MATTHEW 19:26

You work a full-time job. You're tired in the evenings. You already wake up early, getting your workout in and taking some time to pray or read. When will you take on this side gig? When will you find time to sketch your ideas or write your poems or plan or play or dream?

Fitting one more thing into your schedule feels impossible.

And not in the exaggerated sense. You *really do* have a tight schedule. It's not just work, but it's taking the kids to school, date night with your spouse, doing laundry, tending to the yard, taking care of your pets, and honoring volunteer commitments. Maybe it's even all those things on the same day!

When a rich young man walked up to Jesus, he asked, "Teacher, what good deed must I do to have eternal life?" (Matthew 19:16). Jesus responded by telling the young man to "keep the commandments." *I'm doing all of that*, the man replied. *What's next?* "What do I still lack?" (v. 20).

If you're asking this question at the end of your long, drawn-out days,

> "Teacher, what good
> deed must I do to
> have eternal life?"
> (Matthew 19:16)

if your days are full yet your life still seems lacking, isn't it time to rethink your schedule? Making time for your creative outlet might make all the difference in the world.

Never forget: with God *all* things are possible.

EXPLORE

Who in your life inspires you? They balance their schedule, make time for what matters, and model what you believe it means to live well. Consider people who take risks; who make time to play; who are curious about the world; who are positive, motivated, and seemingly fearless.

Reach out to someone who fits those characteristics this week. Seek permission to conduct a short interview over coffee or dinner. You can keep this casual, but do prepare a list of questions ahead of time. What do you want to know? What do you admire about their story?

Be sure to ask how they got to this point—it might be that they started in a place very similar to where you are now.

Leave Your Enemies Behind

"Get behind me, Satan! You are a hindrance to me."
MATTHEW 16:23

Sometimes we are our own worst enemy. We talk ourselves into quitting before we even try. Other times there really is an enemy beyond our control. Here are a few enemies to creativity you might encounter along the way:

- *Failure.* This enemy will whisper things in your ear like "It'll never work out" or "You'll never finish." He will do his best to keep you from starting something outside of the norm or what feels comfortable.

- *Criticism.* This enemy wants you to believe every negative thing other people have said about you. She will draw attention to the one bad thing Random Guy on the internet said, instead of the multitude of comments your friends and family have left praising your work.

- *Ignorance.* This enemy reminds you constantly of what you don't know. He wants you to believe that lack of experience and lack of knowledge is a permanent situation, not something that corrects itself over time as you try and learn and grow.

There are others: procrastination, perfectionism, overthinking, apathy. Face all of them the way Jesus faced Peter when he tried to talk Jesus out of walking God's path for Him: "Get away from me, Satan! You are not helping me!" (Matthew 16:23 ERV).

Keep your eyes on God's path and plan.

IMAGINE

An allegory is a story where the characters, places, and events stand for something more than they seem on the surface. Many children's stories are allegories, called fables; the animals in the story represent the lesson they are trying to teach. For instance, in *The Tortoise and the Hare*, the tortoise represents perseverance while the hare represents arrogance.

Choose an enemy from the list above: What animal represents that enemy well? Can you write a short story about how that enemy works in people's lives, trying to steer them off course? You might read a few fables for inspiration. Have fun with this and, of course, be creative!

Two Gifts

"My grace is sufficient for you, for my power is made perfect in weakness."

2 CORINTHIANS 12:9

Whatever enemy you're facing, you're not its first adversary, and you won't be the last.

Inventor Thomas Edison famously failed not once, not ten times, but ten times *one thousand* times. He optimistically responded, "I've successfully found ten thousand ways that will not work."

Pablo Picasso, one of the most treasured artists around the globe, didn't find immediate success. Instead, he faced harsh criticism, being labeled "satanic" and a "schizophrenic," and his technique was cast as "underworld form."[2]

Pulitzer Prize–winning author John Steinbeck faced self-doubt after receiving praise for his work. He wrote: "I am assailed by my own ignorance and inability . . . Sometimes, I seem to do a little good piece of work, but when it is done it slides into mediocrity."[3]

Whatever creative path you're walking, you won't be the first to face fear or failure or criticism or self-doubt. But as a believer, you have two gifts:

Whatever creative path you're walking, you won't be the first to face fear or failure or criticism or self-doubt.

Prayer: "Watch and pray that you may not enter into temptation. The spirit indeed is willing, but the flesh is weak" (Matthew 26:41).

Grace: "My grace is sufficient for you, for my power is made perfect in weakness" (2 Corinthians 12:9).

Pray for God to deliver you. Even if He doesn't, you have His grace to help you overcome. So, whatever you face, remember that countless others have gone before you and many more will follow. You won't be facing it alone.

CONNECT

Often, our situation doesn't seem as troublesome when we open our eyes to what others are facing. This week, open your eyes to those who've said yes to a new venture and to a new location. When you leave what's familiar, it's easy to give into fear because you feel alone.

Do you have a family at your church who has taken this risk?

Have they said yes to God's plan by moving to a new city or country? Write them a note this week, letting them know they are in your prayers. If they are from your city, make your note even sweeter by including a sketch of a favorite spot they'd be familiar with.

SUPPLIES:

- Paper
- Envelope
- Stamp
- Sketch paper (optional)
- Pencil (optional)

The Right Time

"And who knows but that you have come to your royal position for such a time as this?"

ESTHER 4:14 NIV

Why me?

Because you are loved. If you're asking this question, the answer really is that simple. Why would God give you this gift? Why would God give you this opportunity? Because He loves you with an everlasting love and, therefore, continues His faithfulness to you (Jeremiah 31:3).

Why now?

Maybe you think you're too young and haven't spent enough time developing your skills. Maybe you think you're too busy; you'll wait to take on a side gig when you have more time. Maybe you think you're too old, and the opportunity has passed you by.

Here's what you can trust: if God is putting something on your heart—whether it's an idea for a side project or just a notion that you need to

> ## God's plans are for your good.

be more intentional about setting aside time to create, to play, to grow, to connect, to reflect, to embrace, to inspire and be inspired–God deliberately planted that desire because He has plans for you, and His plans are for your good, "to give you a future and a hope" (Jeremiah 29:11).

So, who knows? Maybe right now is exactly the right time for such a change. After all, the God who created you knows exactly what you need and when and why. Trust His leading as you lead a creative life in His footsteps.

CREATE

The first and greatest Creative One is your Father; you inherited creativity from Him. To remind yourself of this truth, create a print of your own footprint. If you have children in your life, invite them to create prints of their feet alongside you. (This can double as a thoughtful gift, but ultimately, it's about reminding you to follow in your heavenly Father's footsteps.)

First, cover the bottom of your foot with washable paint and then place your footprint on the paper. If you're adding a child's footprint, in a different color and on top of your own, place their smaller additional footprint. Around the footprints, add a verse of your choice (suggestions include 1 John 2:6 and Ephesians 2:10).

Hang this print after yours has dried, where you can see it daily; let it inspire you to keep trusting, keep trying, keep creating.

Just as you've been inspired to step out on your own path by studying the works of artists who came before you, your creations will go on to do the same for others. And remember that when we use our gifts and desires to honor God, anything we create is good. He is always working with, in, and through us: nourishing the creative soul within.

SUPPLIES:

- *Paper*
- *Washable paint (two colors)*
- *Permanent marker (or type/print verse onto paper)*
- *Frame (optional)*

Notes

1. "Watching Birds Near Your Home Is Good for Your Mental Health," University of Exeter, February 24, 2017, https://www. exeter.ac.uk/news/featurednews/title_571299_en.html.

2. Tanya Singh, "7 Masterpieces Rejected by Art Critics," Agora Gallery, February 23, 2017, agora-gallery.com/advice/ blog/2017/02/23/art-criticism-masterpieces/.

3. Steinbeck wrote this in *Working Days* (his daily journal posthumously published in 1989). https://www.penguin. com/ajax/books/excerpt/9780140247756.